REPORTERS AROUND THE WORLD

by FRANK K. KELLY

Many famous men and women have been reporters. Many have had adventures in their personal lives equal to any they covered as reporters. Here are seventeen stories of such adventures.

Here you will find Daniel Defoe, the creator of *Robinson Crusoe*, shackled in the pillory, facing a London mob.

Here you will see Dr. Samuel Johnson, trying to catch a ghost in Cock Lane.

Here is Henry Morton Stanley, pursuing Dr. Livingstone into the dark depths of Africa.

Here is Nellie Bly, racing around the world for the *New York World*, Joseph Pulitzer's great paper.

Here is Winston Churchill, escaping from his captors in the Boer War . . . Richard Harding Davis, accused by the Germans of being a British spy . . . Ernest Hemingway, facing death in Italy . . . Winifred Black, begging for help for the flood-wrecked city of Galveston . . . Ernie Pyle, learning the true strength of Americans . . . Hal Boyle, saving a child in the burning capital of Korea.

These are great people — as well as great reporters.

REPORTERS AROUND THE WORLD

REPORTERS
AROUND
THE WORLD

by FRANK K. KELLY

Illustrations by E. Harper Johnson

AN ATLANTIC MONTHLY PRESS BOOK
LITTLE, BROWN AND COMPANY *Boston • Toronto*

LIBRARY OF CONGRESS CATALOG CARD NO. 56-9078

Second Printing

The author wishes to express special gratitude to Hal Boyle, Edward R. Murrow, Marguerite Higgins, Walter Winchell and William L. Laurence for their cooperation in making available material for this book; to Crown Publishers, Inc., for permission to reprint from Ernest Hemingway's Introduction to *Men at War,* copyright 1942, Crown Publishers, Inc.; to the *New York World-Telegram & Sun* and other Scripps-Howard papers for permission to reprint from Ernie Pyle's columns; and to all those who aided him in his researches.

ATLANTIC–LITTLE, BROWN BOOKS
ARE PUBLISHED BY
LITTLE, BROWN AND COMPANY
IN ASSOCIATION WITH
THE ATLANTIC MONTHLY PRESS

*Published simultaneously in Canada
by Little, Brown & Company (Canada) Limited*

PRINTED IN THE UNITED STATES OF AMERICA

To My Sons,
Terence and Stephen

Contents

The Brave and the Bold

Many famous men and women have been reporters. Many have had adventures in their personal lives — adventures equal to any they covered as reporters.

Here are seventeen stories of such adventures, encountered by men and women who were both brave and bold. Some stayed reporters all their lives. Others went on to win fame as novelists, as explorers, as political leaders. Others are still shaping their careers, still making headlines.

Here you will find Daniel Defoe, the creator of *Robinson Crusoe,* shackled in the pillory, facing a London mob.

Here you will see Dr. Samuel Johnson, trying to catch a ghost in Cock Lane.

Here is Henry Morton Stanley, pursuing Dr. Livingstone into the dark depths of Africa.

Here is Nellie Bly, racing around the world for the *New York World,* Joseph Pulitzer's great paper.

Here is Winston Churchill, escaping from his captors

in the Boer War . . . Richard Harding Davis, accused by the Germans of being a British spy . . . Ernest Hemingway, facing death in Italy . . . Winifred Black, begging for help for the flood-wrecked city of Galveston . . . Ernie Pyle, learning the true strength of Americans . . . Hal Boyle, saving a child in the burning capital of Korea.

These are the brave and the bold. Their courage and their daring made them great as people — as well as reporters.

FRANK K. KELLY

REPORTERS AROUND THE WORLD

1 | Man in the Pillory — the Ordeal of Defoe

Under a blazing sun, in the last days of July, 1703, Daniel Defoe rode in the prison cart from Newgate Gaol to the pillory before the Royal Exchange in Cornhill. His hands bound, his head bowed, he stood silent in the jolting cart, rattling through the cobbled streets of the London he loved. He heard the cries of the street vendors, the loud voices of tough young Cockneys swaggering and arguing, the rising racket of the London throngs.

He was glad to be out of the filth and the darkness of the Newgate jail, to see the sun again, to be away from the moans of the ragged prisoners in that evil place. He had spent two hard months there, surrounded by thieves and murderers, hopeless debtors and desperate political prisoners. He had seen men and women go forth to be executed for stealing bread and meat; he had heard the screams of men being whipped and tortured by the jailers.

It was a great joy to be under the open sky, in the city where he had grown up to manhood, in the capital of England. It was a great joy to see the independent faces of free Englishmen, who showed their sense of rough liberty in every stride they took, in the jokes they called to one another.

Yet he knew this might be the last day of his life. The very people he loved might destroy him.

When he stood in the pillory, everything would depend upon the mood of the mob in the streets. His friends had assured him they would be there to rally the people, to start the crowd singing one of his songs. He counted on his friends; he was sure they would not fail him. But no man could tell what the street crowd would do.

He had no illusions about himself or his fellow countrymen. He knew they could be cruel as well as brave. He had seen other men suffering in the pillory.

When he saw the platform and the wooden shackles waiting for him, he flinched a little. He had proved his courage in many a fight, with his fists as a boy, with his sword as a man. He had fought in the front ranks of the army that rallied to the Duke of Monmouth during the rebellion of 1685. He had risked death and disgrace by joining the forces of Prince William of Orange when William and Mary marched upon London in 1688.

So he was not a weak man or a cowardly man. Yet the sight of the pillory almost broke his spirit. No man, however strong, however courageous, could stand shackled in that wooden frame and win a battle with a London mob.

People were pouring toward the platform from the narrow streets all around the Royal Exchange. Shouts rose below him: "There he is, lads! There's Defoe!"

He closed his eyes for a moment. His legs trembled, his knees loosened under him. He almost fell.

Then a surge of strength came to him — the surge he always felt when he seemed to be at the end of his endurance. It had sustained him when he had lost his position as a successful merchant, when he had toppled into the depths of bankruptcy. He had felt it again when Monmouth's army had been trapped and defeated, and he had escaped through a swamp, hunted by the King's troops. He had been suddenly certain that he would be able to take whatever he had to take.

He felt it now. He was an Englishman and he would not quail before his fellow men. He was being viciously punished for speaking with a bold tongue, for writing too defiantly. He had to take his punishment, but he did not have to yield his spirit to his oppressors. He raised his head.

"Say now, Defoe!" came a cry from the crowd below him. "Who's a true-born Englishman?"

As the guards seized his arms and his head, he looked

full at the pillory. It had in its very shape all the brutality of tyrants. It was a hideous thing, a squat and ugly machine, cunningly constructed to crush a man in body and soul.

His arms were thrust through the holes provided for them. His shoulders were forcibly bent, his neck was stooped, his head was lowered into the position of a penitent. He heard the locks being fastened around him.

How strong his words must have been, to have made his judges so angry. How he must have stung them with his pamphlets, with his verses telling them that a true-born Englishman was a mongrel, with his ironic advice to exterminate dissenters if they truly believed dissenters were so dangerous to the public safety. How he must have galled them with his bitter honesty, to make them pass so terrible a sentence upon him — a sentence which might lead now to his death.

There in the pillory, he saw people still streaming toward the Royal Exchange from every direction. Old men and young men, women with their children were hurrying to gaze upon the spectacle of Dan Defoe, the pamphleteer, exposed for the blows of any who might want to strike at him.

When the warrant had been issued in January for his arrest, he had known that his enemies in Queen Anne's government were out to smash him. He had felt that his only hope was to go into hiding and plead for the Queen's mercy. He had done so — and from his hiding places he had sent letters asking for clemency. He had called upon his friends for help.

But Speaker Harley in the House of Commons had declared it was "absolutely necessary for the service of the Government" to find the author of the pamphlet called *The Shortest Way with Dissenters*. It was considered a subversive document. Copies of it were ripped from the printer's hands and ordered to be burned by the common hangman.

"God save me," Defoe said to himself, looking down at the crowd gathering around the platform. He tried to see whether any of his friends were there.

His head bent, he remembered the day when he had seen the proclamation offering a reward of fifty pounds for information leading to his capture. The reward was advertised in the *Gazette,* with a description of him: "He is a middle-aged, spare man, about forty years old, of a brown complexion, with dark-brown colored hair, but wears a wig; has a hooked nose, a sharp chin, grey eyes, and a large mole near his mouth. . . ." The description was good — no one could fail to see the mole on his face — and the reward was big enough to tempt some people to hunt him.

Yet he had eluded the hunters for five months, moving

from place to place, aided by his friends. Once he had been recognized in Hackney Fields. But he had drawn his sword and forced the man down on both knees and made the fellow swear that if they ever met again the man should shut his eyes till Defoe was half a mile away.

He stared into the jostling crowd, seeking the face of his faithful wife Mary, hoping she would not have come, hoping she would not see him in such a plight. He wanted her to be at home with the children; he did not want her near this hill where he hung in the pillory.

He was sorry now that he had drawn the Government's wrath down upon his friend Jacques, the French weaver. He had been captured in the weaver's house and he knew Jacques had suffered for it. He hated to bring suffering to his friends.

Why had the Queen refused to give him mercy? He had done nothing, except to write what he thought, to paint a picture of things as they seemed to him. Perhaps his letters to the lords around her had never reached her.

Although he did not think he deserved any punishment for letting his pen run free, he had offered to serve in the Queen's cavalry without payment, to fight in the Netherlands for her. He had written to one of the ministers: "Without doubt, my Lord, I shall die there much more to her service than in a prison." But no answer had come.

Suddenly his thoughts were interrupted. Suddenly a quiver of excitement shot through him. He saw good friends of his, good friends pushing through the crowd, forming a ring around the platform. They gestured to him, they lifted their hands in salutes, and he saw they carried bundles of pamphlets.

"Who'll sing Dan Defoe's 'Hymn to the Pillory'?" a loud voice called, just below him. "Here's a hymn for you, friends, written in the hell hole of Newgate, a song for true-born Englishmen."

People reached out eagerly for the pamphlets containing the hymn. Silver money flashed in the sun. People were buying the hymn he had created in Newgate—the hymn that cried out all his defiance of the lords who had treated him badly, who had punished him unfairly.

Those in the first ranks of the crowd began to sing the verses that voiced his straight accusations of those who should really be in the pillory. With the strength of his heart, writing with the howls of beaten prisoners piercing his Newgate cell, he had denounced stupid military commanders, money-grubbing financiers, swindling stock jobbers, power-grabbing politicians, all men who yielded to their vices and cheated the people.

That was a hymn a London crowd of Cockneys could sing with joy. Their voices made the streets ring with it. They had a chance to sing out, loud and clear, what they thought of many of their lords and masters—and they did.

They roared the ending of the hymn:

> *"Tell them, the men that placed him here*
> *Are scandals to the times!*
> *Are at a loss to find his guilt,*
> *And can't commit his crimes!"*

When they finished, Defoe's friends went into the nearby taverns and returned with tankards of ale and stoups of wine. They drank to the man in the pillory.

"Here's to your health, Dan Defoe!" they shouted. "Here's to a long life for you!"

Girls leaped to the platform and garlanded the pillory with flowers. The guards rushed forward and forced them off, but the flowers stayed there, sweet and soft around him.

"Lord, I thank Thee!" said Daniel Defoe. The weight of the wooden frame around his head was no longer heavy. There were tears on his face, tears of joy he couldn't keep from flowing. "My friends, may you be blessed for your kindness to me this day."

He looked down at his hands, which hung helpless in the wooden stocks. His hands were pinioned now, but in Newgate Gaol his hands had worked for him, writing and writing, shaping the words of the song that saved him.

All that day, while he stood in the pillory under the sun and under a late drizzle of rain, the crowd was on his side.

Once he saw some men going through the lines, giving people broadsheets, and he heard voices muttering, "Read about his crimes, he's a damned dirty seditious dog." The agents of the Queen's ministers were at work, trying to turn the throng into a mob, trying to start a hailstorm of stones that would finish him.

But the crowd was not swayed. The people knew he had earned his bread with the sweat of his hands. The people knew he was a true Londoner, one who had survived the Great Plague and the Great Fire, one who loved the city and his fellow Londoners. They would not stone him.

When he was taken down at last, his limbs were stiff, his feet were like pieces of wood. He had a hard time walking to the prison cart. Then the crowd raised a final cheer and his heart rose.

He saw a horseman riding off; he knew it was one of the Queen's agents, going to tell the ministers that Daniel Defoe had met triumph, not death, in the pillory at Cornhill.

It was the greatest day of his life. As long as he lived, he would remember the flowers falling around him when he had feared the blows of bricks and stones. As long as he lived, he would remember the London throng singing his hymn, drinking to his health and happiness.

From that day forward, he was one of the most famous men in England. He stood twice more in the pillory — and twice more he was hailed by the people.

Soon afterward, with the aid of a leader of Parliament, he was set free. He rose to become editor of the *London Review,* and to be the creator of *Robinson Crusoe.*

2 | Dr. Johnson and the Cock Lane Mystery

In a narrow dark street called Cock Lane, in a slum section of London, during the winter of 1762, a series of strange noises — knockings and scratchings — sounded in a tiny room of an old dark house. The house was occupied by the family of a man named Parsons, who was the parish clerk of St. Sepulchre's Church in West Smithfield.

In that tiny room was a short table with a single lighted candle. Next to the table was a small bed in which a wide-eyed girl of twelve cowered and quaked beneath a mound of blankets. She was the daughter of Mr. Parsons, and he had spread the story through London that his daughter's person was haunted by the tormented spirit of a gentlewoman who had been murdered.

London in that age was always echoing with stories of ghosts and mysteries and wonders. The girl in Cock Lane became the talk of the town. The street where she lived soon became crowded night and day with curiosity-seekers, with muttering old women and poking old men, with rich people and poor people who had nothing better to do than hunt for sensations. They were hoping to see the ghost walk.

One night a handsome coach, pulled by four white horses, came galloping up to the entrance of Cock Lane. From the coach descended one of the heirs to the throne of England — the Duke of York — accompanied by Lady Northumberland, Lady Mary Coke, Lord Hertford, and Horace Walpole.

"Make way for the Duke!" someone cried, recognizing a member of the royal family.

The onlookers around the steps of the house pulled aside reluctantly. The Duke and his party pushed their way to the girl's room, where they found dozens of Londoners packed in around her. Some of the ghost-seekers were tumbling over the girl's bed. The heat and the stench were too much for the Duke, and he was told that the ghost would not manifest itself until seven in the morning.

The Duke and his accompanying lords and ladies fled from the spot, hastening to their coach and hurrying away. Royalty had found no answer to the mystery in Cock Lane.

Not long afterward, a huge man with reddish hair and a large nose, wearing a battered cloak and walking with slow heavy strides, came into the lane between the hours of eleven and twelve at night. He was Dr. Samuel

Johnson, the poet and lexicographer, assigned to investigate the puzzle by the *Gentleman's Magazine.*

Dr. Johnson had no particular relish for such assignments, but he undertook them because he was hungry. He was not yet recognized as a genius and a great scholar. He was simply a reporter who needed money in his pockets.

With quiet force, Dr. Johnson went in to the house of Mr. Parsons. His bulk, his dignity, and his strength got him through the crowd on the stairs. He went in and stood at the foot of the bed, and saw that the child was shaking the bedclothes with fright.

After watching for half an hour, Dr. Johnson could see no visible evidence of a deceit. But he was not satisfied with the idea that any supernatural spirit was at work.

He left the house thoughtfully, and returned the next night with an informal committee to investigate the matter. The committee consisted of two or three clergymen — including the well-known exposer of fraud, the Rev. Dr. Douglas, who later became Bishop of Salisbury — and about twenty other persons, including two Negroes.

They thoroughly examined the bed, the bedclothes, the floor, and the area surrounding the bed. Then the child, with her sister, was placed again in the bed. Dr. Johnson stood once more at the end of it, closely observing.

Mr. Parsons explained that the ghost answered questions by knocking or scratching. An affirmative answer was expressed by one knock, a negative by two. If the ghost was displeased by a question, there would be a furious scratching.

The knockings and scratchings previously heard had already been interpreted to mean that the ghost was the spirit of a lady named Fanny who had supposedly been given arsenic by a neighbor named Mr. Kent with whom she and Parsons had once lodged.

On the night when Dr. Johnson stood in the room with his committee, the ghost was extremely talkative. In an article printed later, Dr. Johnson reported the questions asked of the girl and the replies received.

"Was your disturbance caused by any ill-treatment from Mr. Kent?" she was asked.

A single knock replied, "Yes."

"Were you brought to an untimely end by poison?" "Yes."

"How long before your death was the poison given?"

Through a series of knockings, interpreted by Mr. Parsons, the answer was obtained: "Three hours."

"What about the person called Carrots — a servant — would she be able to give information about the poison?"

The answer came promptly: "Yes."

"How long before your death had you told Carrots that you were poisoned?"

"One hour," came the reply.

The little servant girl called Carrots, who was in the room, declared that Miss Fanny had not said anything about being poisoned, but had been completely speechless for hours before her death.

The questions were resumed.

"How long did Carrots live with you?"

"Three or four days," came the reply.

The servant girl said this was true.

"If the accused man should be taken up, would he confess?"

The answer came at once: "Yes."

"Would she be at ease in her mind if the man was hanged?"

"Yes," came the reply.

"How long would it be before he would be executed?"

Through another series of knockings, the answer was given: "Three years."

The ghost of Fanny, if such the spirit proved to be, was then asked how many clergymen were in the room.

"Three," came the reply.

"How many Negroes?"

"Two."

"What was the color of a watch held up by one of the clergymen — white, yellow, blue, or black?"

"Black."

The watch was in a black shagreen case. The answer given by the knockings seemed to be correct.

When the committee, headed by the Rev. Dr. Douglas, left the girl's room, some of them were visibly impressed. Dr. Johnson's opinion was sought as they walked slowly from the dark little house in Cock Lane.

The big man snorted. "Why, I believe it is the most arrant nonsense, sir, arrant nonsense!"

"But how could that small girl give the replies to all those questions?" a committee member said.

"Through her father, sir," Dr. Johnson growled. "The clerk Parsons is well acquainted with Mr. Kent and was well acquainted with Miss Fanny. There was a quarrel between Mr. Parsons and Mr. Kent. There is enmity between them."

"If there is fraud here, it should be exposed," said the Rev. Dr. Douglas. "Already there is talk of calling Mr. Kent up for trial."

"Indeed, sir, the exposure of such a fraud is noble work," Dr. Johnson said. "Let us put the little girl to a test that will not harm her but will expose any imposture."

Dr. Douglas agreed. "I think it is our duty to do so.

Mr. Kent's reputation, perhaps his life, now are at stake."

It was decided that the test would be held at the home of the Rev. Mr. Aldrich of Clerkenwell, who had expressed his readiness to have it conducted there.

The supposed spirit of Miss Fanny had publicly promised, under earlier questioning, that it would attend one of the gentlemen of the committee into the vault under the church of St. John, Clerkenwell, where Miss Fanny's body rested. There, the spirit said, it would give a loud knock as an indication of her presence in the coffin.

On the night of February 1, some gentlemen of high rank and standing assembled at the home of the Rev. Mr. Aldrich. Dr. Johnson was with them, making notes of everything that happened.

At about ten o'clock the gentlemen went upstairs to the bedchamber where the little Parsons girl had been put to bed by several ladies. They sat around the bed for more than an hour, watching the girl in complete silence. She lay very still and looked back at them, her glance moving from face to face.

"As I told you, gentlemen, nothing will happen," Dr. Johnson said.

No sounds were heard in the room, except the rapid breathing of the little girl and an occasional cough from one of the gentlemen watching her.

Shortly before midnight the gentlemen rose, convinced that Johnson was right, and left the bedchamber.

Just as they got into the hall, however, two of the ladies who had remained with the girl came rushing out to them.

"We heard the sounds!" the ladies cried. "Knockings and scratchings!"

"Were you keeping your eyes closely upon her?" Dr. Johnson demanded.

"No, we were looking after you. But we heard the sounds."

When the gentlemen returned to the room, the girl declared that she felt the spirit like a mouse upon her back. She was required to hold her hands out of the bed.

Although she protested that the spirit was running up and down her back, she was not allowed to slip her hands under the bedclothes. And there were no more scratchings or knockings.

"It is now past midnight," said Dr. Johnson. "It is approaching one o'clock. Let us go down into the vault and see if any spirit knocks upon the coffin there."

The whole group of gentlemen then went into the church. The gentleman to whom the supposed spirit had promised to give a sign of recognition went into the vault with one companion and stood near the coffin of Miss Fanny.

The people in the church and the two men in the vault stood absolutely still for a long time, to give the spirit an opportunity to speak, if any spirit lingered there.

One of the group then called out, "Spirit, if you are here, perform your solemn promise. Give a knock from the coffin. Make your presence known among us."

The stillness was not broken. There was no knock, no scratch, no sound at all.

Then Mr. Kent, the accused man, who was in the church, asked for the right to go into the vault and stand by the coffin of Miss Fanny. He declared his innocence and his confidence that there would be no sound of accusation when he entered the vault.

Mr. Kent walked down into the vault, accompanied by several other men. The supposed spirit did not stir. There was no knocking, no sign of disturbance at Mr. Kent's presence.

"It is a fraud, gentlemen," said Dr. Johnson. "There was no ghost in Cock Lane."

"I shall seek justice for the damage done me by this fakery," declared Mr. Kent.

"You should, sir," said Dr. Johnson. "You have been grievously injured by this imposture."

The group returned to the home of the Rev. Mr. Aldrich and called Mr. Parsons in for questioning.

"Come, sir, acknowledge that Miss Fanny died of

smallpox, as the medical records show," Dr. Johnson said. "She was never poisoned by Mr. Kent or any other man. And there was never a supernatural spirit in your little girl's room."

Mr. Parsons vigorously denied any knowledge of any fraud. The girl would make no confession.

Later it was discovered that she had taken a piece of wood to bed with her and had produced the knockings with that instrument, which she had concealed from all searchers. It was found that the quarrel between her father and Mr. Kent had been bitter and deep, and she had not hesitated to help her father in getting Mr. Kent into trouble.

After the failure of the "ghost" to appear in the vault in St. John's Church in Clerkenwell, Mr. Kent called upon the authorities to take action against Mr. Parsons and his accomplices for plotting against his life and his reputation.

Mr. Parsons was found guilty, placed in the pillory, and then sent to prison for two years. His wife and a woman named Mary Frazer, who had interpreted some of the "spirit" messages, received briefer terms. Two other persons who had taken part in the fraud were fined a total of six hundred pounds.

Reporting the results of his investigation in the *Gentle-*

man's Magazine, Dr. Johnson urged his readers to beware of "the renowned Society of Ghostmongers."

"Look out for the managers behind the screens," Johnson said. "They are no spirits. They are as surely clothed with flesh and blood as you yourselves are, only guarding most cautiously against the light, because they too well know their deeds are evil. . . ."

3 | Young Charles Dickens Finds His Father in Prison—and Becomes a Crusader Against Debtors' Jails

THE BOY with the fair hair and the quick, sensitive face worked very fast, his nimble fingers flying. He had a row of blacking-pots before him on a shelf; there seemed to be an endless number of them. It was his job to tie up the pots in oil paper and blue paper, and then to paste labels on the wrappings. He sat in a corner of a room on the first floor of a ramshackle house on the London water front.

The floor under him was split and decayed, and there were rats in the walls and rats squeaking and scuffling in the cellars below him. He worked very fast to take his mind off the sound of the rats, the dirt and the smells of the warehouse, the horrible place where he had to be, the misery of his life.

Three other boys did similar jobs, but he said little to them and they paid little attention to him, except to joke now and then about his ways of talking and his airs of being "a young gentleman." But one of them, a large boy named Bob Fagin who wore a paper cap, was kind to him and tried to show him short cuts on the job.

When he had the sharp pains in his side and the world began to whirl around him, when he got so dizzy he had to roll from his chair to the floor, Bob Fagin took him into a back room and put warm cloths on him and stayed with him until the spasms were over. He was grateful to Bob Fagin. Later he used Bob's name in a book called *Oliver Twist* and gave Bob a kind of immortality — although he did give the name to a villain who bore no real resemblance to kindly, friendly Fagin.

None of the boys in the warehouse knew much about him, except that his name was Charles Dickens and he was short and slim for a boy of twelve.

Today he worked faster than he had ever done before, because he did not want to think at all. He did not want to think about what had happened to his family, what had happened to his father. He hoped none of the boys in the warehouse knew about that.

He felt utterly neglected and hopeless, but he was too proud to tell his grief to anyone. He had been separated from his family, he had been put into a lodginghouse, because his father could no longer afford to keep a home together. His father's debts had dragged the family down to poverty and disgrace.

Not that he blamed his father. He knew his father was one of the jolliest, kindest men alive. When he had been very sick, his father had stayed up with him night after night. His father loved to hear him sing comic songs; his father was proud of him and let the whole world know it.

Bob Fagin, passing the chair where young Dickens sat with his fingers racing over the labels, looked at him anxiously.

"What's the matter, Charlie?" asked Fagin. "Not sick again now, are you, lad?"

"I'm all right now."

"You're a bit blue around the gills, lad. It'll be time to quit soon. I'll walk home with you."

"Thank you, Bob," Dickens said, gulping. "You don't have to do that. You want to get to your own house in time for dinner."

"I'll go without my dinner if I have to," Fagin said, with a smile. "I've done it before. But they'll keep something on the back of the stove for me, Charlie."

Fagin went down the stairs to the cellars, and young Dickens sat rigid in his chair, not knowing what to say. He could not tell Bob Fagin that he was going to see his father in the Marshalsea Prison when his work was done.

When the wrapping and pasting was finished for the day, Fagin insisted again that he would accompany young Dickens through the streets near the water front.

"Bob, I tell you I'm all right," Dickens said, after a few minutes of walking. "Please get home to your dinner. I'm grateful to you, but I'll feel all the better if you go home now."

Fagin studied him a moment. "As you wish it, lad. You do look a bit more chipper. Another night I'll walk the whole distance with you, if you don't mind."

"Yes, Bob, that will be fine," Dickens said, sighing with relief. If Fagin came with him another night, he would walk Bob far from the place where he really lived — and far from the prison where his father was held.

"Good night, lad."

"Good night," Dickens said.

As soon as Fagin had disappeared around a corner, Dickens turned toward the Marshalsea. He knew his father would be waiting for him.

When he saw the huge stone building where his gay father had come to the end of all his hopes, Dickens had to force himself to take one step after another, dragging his unwilling legs to the entrance. He could not bear to look upon that bleak place without weeping.

The grim building stood south of the Thames in Southwark. It was hundreds of years old. It bore around it a cloud of grime and dirt, and its history was full of human suffering and the wreckage of men's dreams.

Its name was drawn from the title of the Marshal of the King's House, who had the custody of debtors along with other responsibilities. In the Marshalsea, the debtors lived in a twilight state — not chained or locked in vaults as some prisoners were, but confined within its boundaries until their debts were paid or settled. Visitors were allowed to come and go, and the families of some men were permitted to live in the prison with them.

The small, short boy with the fair hair and the thin, hungry face, young Charles Dickens, came slowly to the gates. There was a noise of voices, people were passing in and out, some of the jailers were selling beer and wine. It was a frowzy, clamorous place — a nightmare place for a boy to find his father.

That small, bewildered boy took in everything he heard and saw. He never forgot any of it. He never lost the vision of that prison as he saw it then.

He saw the injustice of putting men into prison for debts. He saw how that form of punishment was both cruel and useless, because the men could not repay what they owed while they lay in prison. He saw what it cost the families of these men, the pain inflicted on their children.

That pain he carried with him through life — through his years as a reporter, his rise to world-wide fame as a novelist, his many days of applause and achievement.

And though he did not know it when he stood before the Marshalsea, he had in him a power of expression that would awaken the conscience of his country to the evils of such prisons. He had in him a power that would clear the way for the destruction of such places. As a reporter and as a novelist, he led a crusade against such jails.

But he did not have any idea of this power then. He thought his world had fallen into pieces. His father — his handsome, laughing father, who loved to have him get up on a table and sing funny songs — had been arrested. His father was behind those walls.

He went into the gatekeeper's lodge, and found his father there. They could not speak. They embraced.

"Come up to my room," the father said, choking.

As they went up the crowded stairs, surrounded by strangers who were jostling them apart, they both wept.

Years afterward, when he was one of the great men of England and one of the great writers of the world, Charles Dickens wrote the story of that meeting.

The shock and sorrow he felt then went into his writing and made the world feel the agony of a small boy who had found his beloved father in prison.

The father believed the sun had set upon his life forever.

"We . . . cried very much," wrote Charles Dickens

later, and he wept again over the memory. "And he told me, I remember, to take warning by the Marshalsea, and to observe that if a man had twenty pounds a year and spent nineteen pounds, nineteen shillings and sixpence, he would be happy: but that a shilling spent the other way would make him wretched. I see the fire we sat before, now: with two bricks inside the rusted grate, one on each side, to prevent its burning too many coals. . . ."

The small, tired boy believed that his heart had been broken, that he could never feel the brightness of the sun again.

His father begged him to stay and share the prison dinner, and then discovered there was no knife and fork for him.

Years later, Dickens painted in words the scene he found in the room above, where he was dispatched to borrow what he needed. He wrote:

> I was sent up to "Captain Porter" in the room overhead, with Mr. Dickens's compliments, and I was his son, and could he, Captain P, lend me a knife and fork?
>
> Captain Porter lent the knife and fork, with his compliments in return. There was a very dirty lady in his little room; and two wan girls, his daughters, with shock heads of hair. I thought I should not like to have borrowed Captain Porter's comb. The Captain himself was in last extremity of shabbiness; and if I could draw at all, I would draw an accurate portrait of the old, old,

brown great-coat he wore, with no other coat below it.
His whiskers were large. I saw his bed, rolled up in a
corner; and what plates, and dishes and pots he had, on
a shelf; and I knew (God knows how) that the two
girls with the shock heads were Captain Porter's natural
children, and that the dirty lady was not married to Captain P. My timid, wondering station on his threshold
was not occupied more than a couple of minutes, I dare
say; but I came down again to the room below with all
this as surely in my knowledge, as the knife and fork
were in my hand.

He had the quick perception of the born reporter. He
missed no detail in the room. Even though he was
saddened and stunned by the prison, his eyes and his mind
were working swiftly.

He found release from the pain of his experiences in
life by telling them to other people, plainly and vividly,
so that everything which happened to him was important
and exciting.

With this gift, he could not be crushed.

The warehouse on the river, where he spent his days in
labor he hated; the rats on the stairs, squeaking and
scuffling; the cries of the jailers at the Marshalsea, selling
wine and gin, beer and ale; the tears of his father; the
Captain and the dirty lady and the two little girls in the
dirty room — all these things became part of him, and

through him the world saw the sadness and the strangeness of life.

When he found his father in prison, he thought his heart had been broken. But he did not know the power he had in his mind and his heart. He did not know that everything he touched with his pen one day would shine with immortality. And the crusade against debtors' prisons which he helped to lead eventually destroyed those places of suffering.

4 | Stanley Pursues Livingstone to the Heart of Africa

THE HILL AHEAD was steep, jagged with rocks, covered with jungle growths. Staggering under their burdens, the line of black men approaching it groaned and faltered. The heat of the African day was stifling around them. They halted.

The gaunt white man at the end of the line pushed his way forward, gripping his musket.

"No rest yet," said the white man sharply. He waved his arm toward the hill. "We have hours to go before we rest."

The tall black man in front, the guide who had been leading the bearers along a narrow path, glared at him.

"Too much climb hills, master," the tall black man said, panting. "We rest now. We stop here."

The gaunt white man turned to the bearer nearest to him. "Give me a whip," he said. "This guide needs a whip."

"No, Master Stanley," the tall black man growled. "No whip."

The black man had a musket and he suddenly raised it.

With that weapon close to his throat, Henry Stanley felt the memory of the two years he had spent in Africa rushing through his mind — the years of climbing hill after hill, sweating through the mountains, through the jungles, searching for an old man who might be dead, an old man who was seeking the fountains of Herodotus and the sources of the Nile.

His legs were weary, his whole body was aching with fatigue, he was weak from the fevers he had suffered. He was hundreds of miles from civilization. If he should be killed here, his body would be buried under the jungle grass and no one would ever know what had become of him.

His hunt for Dr. Livingstone could not end here. It could not end until he found the old man, until he fulfilled his mission.

He tensed his muscles to spring for the black man's gun.

Before he could move, one of the bearers leaped forward and knocked the guide's musket aside.

"Bind his hands," Stanley said. "Make him march with us."

He lifted his hand and the line of bearers began to move again — slowly, reluctantly slogging up the steep hill, climbing over the jagged rocks, thrusting through the jungle growths.

Sweat running down into his eyes, his gaunt face lined and worn, Stanley kept up with the pace of the advancing line. Paris was a long way from him now — Paris with its broad boulevards, its dancing flags, its beautiful women.

He had hurried to Paris from Madrid when he got the telegram from James Gordon Bennett, Jr., the publisher of the *New York Herald*. Bennett had called him there "on important business." He had found Bennett, a young man still under thirty like himself, lying in bed in a palatial room in the Grand Hotel.

"I want you to find David Livingstone," Bennett had said. "I don't care what it costs or how long it takes. I'll supply you with all the money you'll need. Find Livingstone."

Dr. David Livingstone, a Scottish missionary, famous for the discovery of Victoria Falls and Lake Nyasa, had gone into Africa in 1866 to attempt to put a stop to the slave trade and to find the sources of the Nile. Nothing had been heard from Livingstone since a message had arrived by bearer from the heart of Africa in May of 1869. The message pleaded for men and supplies.

Bennett had given Stanley the assignment to pursue the missionary into Africa in October, 1869. Now he had been searching for month after month, year after year, and the traces of Livingstone were getting fainter, the hope of coming upon him alive was getting less and less.

But his men went marching on, driven by his determination, and he marched with them. He could not stop, he would not stop. He would never abandon hope, he would never admit defeat.

The crest of the rocky hill was reached, and the column of black men descended into a shallow valley. Another hill loomed beyond the valley. The men took that hill without breaking their strides, and came upon another valley.

Then came the cry from the faithful bearer at the head of the line, the man who had saved Stanley from the guide's gun:

"Caravan, master, caravan coming!"

Stanley hurried forward. He saw a caravan of tribesmen approaching slowly.

He prayed to God that this caravan might bring him news which would give him the courage to go on.

The caravan, composed of eighty Waghua tribesmen, had just left the village of Ujiji on Lake Tanganyika. The tribesmen were driving goats along with them, and were friendly, smiling people. And they brought the news Henry Stanley had prayed for.

He described their coming and what it meant to him in his journal, dated November 3, 1871:

A white man was left by them five days ago at Ujiji. He had the same clothes, had the same color as I have, wears the same shoes, and has hair on his face, only his is white. This is Livingstone! Hurrah for Ujiji!

His men shared his exuberance. To celebrate the great tidings that Dr. Livingstone was still alive, he bought three goats and five gallons of native beer from the tribesmen. He gave his bearers a chance to rest, to have a feast, to sing and rejoice.

After that, he ordered them to resume the march. All went well until he came to the village of Kawanga. His column was blocked by village warriors. Their arrows were ready.

"Must pay tribute, master," said the bearer who had risked death for him. "Chief lives in this village."

Stanley was eager to move ahead. He hated to pay tribute, but he could not take the chance of a battle.

"How much?" he said.

The bearer conferred with the spokesman of the village chief.

"Twelve and a half dhoti, master."

A dhoti was a length of loincloth. Twelve and a half lengths was a high tribute. Stanley hesitated, and gave in.

[41]

"We will pay this tribute, but the people must know that we will pay no more between here and Ujiji," Stanley said.

"Yes, master."

Stanley and his men stayed for the night in the village of Kawanga. The next morning the column got under way with much laughter and much shouting. Everybody was very cheerful.

The country beyond Kawanga was pleasant rolling land, somewhat like the American prairies, and Stanley's men found it easier to march across this land than through the hills and jungles they had passed. They did not groan and grumble. Some of them began to sing.

But when they passed another large village, a party of warriors came out after them.

The warriors caught up with them.

"How dare you pass by without paying tribute to the king of Uhha?" demanded the leader of the war party.

"But we paid it," Stanley said. "We gave twelve and a half dhoti to the chief of Kawanga."

"That is only for himself." The warriors encircled Stanley and his bearers. "You stop and rest at our village until we find out the truth."

Stanley refused to go to the village. After much palaver, the warriors sent messengers back to Uhha and sent other men to Mionvu, another chief living not far from the place where Stanley and his expedition had been halted.

Mionvu came to them, Stanley reported later, wearing a crimson cloth arranged like a toga over his shoulder and a piece of sheeting folded around his head. He shook hands with Stanley and the head bearers, and then sat down upon the ground.

"Why does the white man stand in the road?" asked Mionvu. "The sun is hot. Let him seek the shelter of my village. Does he not know that there is a king in Uhha and that I, Mionvu, am his servant? It is a custom for us to make friends with great men, such as the white man. All Arabs and Wanguana stop here and give us cloth. Does the white man mean to go on without paying?"

Before Stanley could answer, Mionvu gestured to the armed warriors who stood watching.

"I know the white man and his men have guns, and we have but spears and arrows," said Mionvu. "But Uhha is large and has plenty of people. The children of the king are many. If he comes to be a friend to us, he will come to our village, give us something, and then go on his way."

The warriors nodded. Stanley knew that if they wished, they could overcome him and his group of bearers, kill them all, and take what they wanted.

"I will go to the chief's village," Stanley said.

With his bearers, Stanley accompanied Mionvu to the cluster of straw-thatched huts. He was impatient, eager to continue his march, determined to let nothing keep him from coming to the village where Dr. Livingstone might be.

But Mionvu made demands for tribute, which Stanley was afraid to meet, because he knew that then other tribesmen along the line of march would wait for his group and ask for gifts. He had to have supplies in reserve. Yet Mionvu insisted upon sixty dhoti for the king, twelve for Mionvu, three for Mionvu's wife, three each for three subchiefs, one to a subchief's little boy. The total came to eighty-five dhoti, or one good bale of cloth.

Stanley had been on the march for so long now that he had only five bales of trading cloth remaining. If he gave Mionvu one bale, he would have a narrow supply of cloth for the journey to Ujiji. The margin of protection for his caravan would be small.

He argued and bargained with Mionvu for eight hours, although he was desperately anxious to hurry along the trail. But at nightfall he yielded, because he knew he would have no peace in Mionvu's village if he did not yield.

After he gave Mionvu the exact amounts of cloth the chief had demanded, Mionvu assured him that he would not have to pay any more tributes while he traveled in the land of Uhha.

"I cannot pay many more such tributes," he said.

He told his men to prepare their beds and stay for the night in the village of Mionvu. Triumphant, the chief was friendly and smiling. Stanley knew the village would be a safe place for at least one night's rest.

The next day, all went well for four hours of marching. Then the line of bearers came to the village of Kahirigi, governed by Mionvu's brother.

Mionvu's brother proved to be as greedy as Chief Mionvu, asking for thirty dhoti as soon as Stanley's men had pitched his tent at the edge of the village. Stanley was willing to give any quantity of trading cloth to smooth his way to Ujiji, but his array of trading bales had diminished to the danger point. He argued with the chief of Kahirigi for five hours, and finally had to pay twenty-six dhoti.

By the time the bargain was reached, night had fallen. Stanley closed his tent, lighted his pipe, and began to think hard. It was time to give battle, or to discover some way of escaping from this territory without granting any additional bribes.

Yet he had learned that there was no jungle ahead of him where his caravan might evade war parties. If he stayed upon the road he had been following, he had to pass with his men over bare plains where his whole group of bearers would be easy targets for the arrows of marauding tribesmen.

He called in the chief bearer, who had become his guide.

"This land of Uhha is a trap for us," Stanley said. "You led us here. You must help us to find a better road."

The guide bowed his dark head. They sat in silence for a moment. Then the guide spoke eagerly.

"Mguana! Mguana can help us."

"Who is he?" demanded Stanley.

"He is slave to Thani bin Abdullah," the guide said. "I get him. He knows all this land of Uhha."

The guide slipped from the tent and returned soon with Mguana, a small, sharp-faced man.

"Mguana, I will give you cloth if you will help us," Stanley said. "Help us to get out of Uhha without paying more tribute."

Mguana was somber. "It is a hard thing to do, master, unless your men will obey your word and do everything you tell them to do."

"They will obey me," Stanley said.

His bearer-guide nodded. "That is true, Mguana."

"Then I will show you a road," Mguana said. "You must pay me twelve dhoti now."

[46]

Stanley gave him the cloth.

"I will come late in the night," Mguana said. "We go then."

Two and a half hours after midnight, Stanley and his men stole silently around the thatched huts. Mguana opened the gates in the village wall. One by one, Stanley and his bearers filed out as quickly as possible.

There were no signs of any villagers. There was a bright moon shining upon the African land, but none of the people in Kahirigi seemed to be awake. No alarm was given.

In the glow of the moon Stanley saw the small man, Mguana, leading the way across a burned plain in a southerly direction. Mguana then turned westward, parallel with the main road, and led the group hour after hour for nearly six hours.

After this marching, Stanley and his bearers found themselves in a thick jungle.

"Jungle miles around this place," Mguana said, as he left them. "Stay in jungle. Keep on path."

Stanley kept the men moving, after a brief halt for breakfast. Through that whole day and through another night, the men moved quietly through the jungle. Mguana had promised to show them a path which avoided villages, and Mguana had kept his promise.

While the caravan was crossing a shallow river, the wife

of one of the bearers, walking with her husband, shrieked that a crocodile had bitten her.

The chief bearer came running to Stanley. "No crocodile here, master. You must stop her noises, master. Villages may be near."

Stanley knew the lives of his men and the fate of his expedition were at stake.

"Stop that noise!" he called to her. "Do you want your husband to die, and all these men with him?"

But she was hysterical and could not stop. Stanley had her gagged. Her arms were tied behind her, and a cord went from her waist to that of her husband. The husband declared he would keep her quiet.

The expedition then got under way again, the men stepping softly through the darkness, every man listening for the sounds of approaching warriors. The hours went by, and no shouts came, no arrows hurtled among them. They had been lucky; the woman's shrieks had not aroused the villagers near them.

After another day's march, they went through a narrow ravine and descended a hill into the land of Ukaranga — beyond the territory of the warlike Wahha tribesmen.

"Safe now, master," said the chief bearer. The tired black men in the long column gave shouts of joy.

Stanley faced them. He saw their weariness, the droop of their shoulders, the sweat on their dark bodies. He was tired, too — tired in his very bones. But the excitement of the pursuit was greater than his tiredness.

"Let us march a few hours more," Stanley urged them. The men were silent. "Tomorrow we shall see the white man at Ujiji, and who knows but this may be the man we are seeking? Let us go on, and after tomorrow we shall have fish for dinner and many days' rest afterwards, every day eating the fish of the Tanganyika." He sniffed the air. "I think I smell the Tanganyika fish even now."

The men began to shout and cheer. Some cried, "Very well, master." Some said, *"Hyah, Barak-Allah"* — Onward, and the blessing of God be on you.

Stanley set the pace at the hard, quick rate of four miles an hour. The expedition marched six hours at this pace. The men were worn down almost to the limits of their endurance, but the caravan kept marching on.

A village came in sight.

"Unfurl the flags," Stanley ordered.

The American and Zanzibar flags were lifted on poles and began to flutter in the wind.

When the expedition approached the house of the chief of Ukaranga, the flags and the guns carried by Stanley's column were seen by the people. The villagers and their chief rushed from their huts and headed for the woods.

The chief bearer in Stanley's column called to them. Their shouts of fear came back.

"There is a bandit named Mirambo," the bearer explained. "He has many robbers with him. These people think we are Mirambo's robbers."

The villagers were calmed, and soon returned with gifts of goats and beer.

"We shall feast here," Stanley said. "In the morning we will go to Ujiji."

He saw that his men were hungry and thirsty, and he could not drive them any farther that day. It was another postponement — and after two years of disappointments, of hope and despair, every postponement was a blow to him. But the men had to rest, the men had to eat, whether he felt the need for rest and food or not.

Yet he was aware of what might happen. Livingstone might die or disappear again before he reached Ujiji. He refused to think of it. He would not let the thought of failure into his mind.

At dawn he rose and gave the command for every man in the column to put on clean clothes. His sun helmet was whitened with chalk and a new cloth was folded around it. His boots were carefully oiled. He wore his white flannel trousers.

When he led his men into Ujiji, he wanted to present the best appearance he could. He wanted the people who saw him there to realize that he was a man of dignity, even in the jungle.

After two hours of marching on that day, the expedition came to the crest of a hill. There below lay the gray waters of Lake Tanganyika.

Stanley later described the lake as "a grand inland sea, bounded westward by an appalling and black-blue range of mountains, and stretching north and south without bounds."

The column moved onward. At last the chief bearer glanced ahead and cried, "We are near Ujiji, master."

"How far?" asked Stanley, his voice leaping.

"About a mile, master."

"Commence firing," Stanley said. "Pass the command along."

The men pointed their muskets toward the sky. Down went the ramrods, sending charges home to the breeches. Volley after volley went banging toward the clouds.

The guides in the vanguard of the column waved the poles carrying the flags. The chief guide blew his horn. The sound of the horn rang out above the firing of the muskets.

Stanley was sure that his long pursuit was coming to an end. After all the fevers, struggles, dangers of his two years in Africa, he was close to the man he sought. He knew he was about to see the face of Dr. Livingstone, the

missing missionary he had hunted so tirelessly, so persistently, in the Dark Continent.

Here is the final moment, as he described it in his dispatch for the *New York Herald:*

We have at last entered the town. There are hundreds of people around me — I might say thousands without exaggeration, it seems to me. It is a grand triumphal procession. As we move, they move. All eyes are drawn towards us. The expedition at last comes to a halt; the journey is ended for a time; but I alone have a few more steps to make.

There is a group of the most respectable Arabs, and as I come nearer I see the white face of an old man among them. He has a cap with a gold band around it, his dress is a short jacket of red blanket cloth, and his pants — well, I didn't observe. I am shaking hands with him. We raise our hats, and I say:

"Dr. Livingstone, I presume?"

And he says, "Yes."

Finis coronat opus. [The end crowns the work.]

Henry Morton Stanley, reporter for the *Herald,* had finished the longest man hunt any reporter had ever undertaken in his time.

5 | Decision in the Wilderness: Mark Twain's Long March

H<small>IS PACK STRAPPED</small> to his back, his pistol hooked in his belt, his slouch hat pulled low upon his head, Sam Clemens stepped from the cabin he had shared with Dan Twing through long months of toil and failure. There was a midnight stillness in the barren hills around him. The sky over Nevada was dusty with the pale light of a million stars.

He was a lanky man, red-bearded, with a keen and reckless face. He had nothing in the world but the clothes and blankets he carried and a handful of silver in one pocket. He had come to Nevada to make his million, and here he was, a miner who had never had the break he needed, a rambler who had never landed in the place where he belonged.

Behind the cabin Dan Twing's dog barked a farewell. Sam Clemens glanced back once at the shack, he raised a hand and rubbed his face, and then he plunged ahead. The August darkness was cool and clear, but he saw no answers in the stars to the questions that plagued him:

What kind of a man should he be? What was he going to do with his life?

The mountains of Nevada huddled in their massive ranks on the horizon, immense and darkly distant. The faint glow from the stars and the moon fell upon the range of desolate hills where he had tried so hard to get rich — the blasted hills of Esmeralda, pitted with holes, pocked by the picks and shovels of miners as hungry as himself, seeking the wealth hidden in the earth.

To be a finder, that was what he had wanted to be. To find the exact right spot and strike it at the right minute — and see the ground gush silver into his hands. Just once he believed he had done it, and then the claim he had staked out had been taken away from him by tougher men than he. He had lost his chance.

Now he was sick of living on barley, beans, and beef. He was tired of swinging a pick and hitting rock and sand. He'd had enough of fighting claim-jumpers. He had spent enough of his brother's money and his own money, trying to be a prospector, trying to be a millionaire. He had done all the mining he intended to do.

But he had Nevada in his blood. He wasn't ready to quit and trot home to Missouri. He didn't want to leave this state. The sky was so big. The mountains were so mighty. The world was wide out here.

Walking toward the dark mountains, he thought of that

lake he had reached with Johnny Kinney, after the tremendous climb from Carson City. It glittered in his memory like a blue diamond — brilliant, pure, beautiful, beyond any price a man could name.

He took in the cool, clean air and he felt like a giant in the Western night. Maybe he'd go to Lake Tahoe and build a hut there; maybe he'd live in a shack on that bright blue shore. He went tramping through the wilderness, restless, swinging his long arms, forgetting the weight of his pack. He wasn't sad, he wasn't sorry for what he had tried to do; he was just moving on.

Maybe Johnny Kinney and he should have been timber cutters. That would have been a good life. Maybe they should have stayed at the edge of Lake Tahoe, in that timeless valley encircled by snow-capped peaks. If it hadn't been for that damned fire, the fire that broke out when his back was turned, they might have kept their timber claim, they might have stayed at Lake Tahoe.

That fire went so fast, with such fury, there was no way of smothering it. It roared in the pines, it burned through the forest, it ate everything it touched. Johnny and he couldn't halt it.

While he walked beneath the stars, his mind leaped back to the day when Johnny and he had put notices on trees near the shining lake, claiming three hundred acres of yellow pine for S. Clemens and J. Kinney. That had been a day of pride for both of them.

After they had posted their notices they had the job of fencing in their land to make their claim secure. They cut down trees here and there, and built a kind of rough fence around the outer borders of the thick-timbered acres. Then they built a brushwood shack and called it a house, to show they had a habitation on their claimed land.

The fire had devoured the brushwood hut, the rude fence, and much of the timber. Johnny and he had retreated to Carson City. They had planned to go back, they had been positive they were still going to be timber cutters.

But he had caught the mining fever. He saw wagons filled with ore, sometimes with chunks of gold and silver, being driven through the dusty streets of Carson City. The men in the stores and the saloons talked of nothing but the riches waiting to be discovered in the hills.

And he had always been an explorer in his heart, from the time of his boy days in Hannibal, when he had crawled into caves along the Mississippi. After he had gotten tired of being a printer's devil, after he had been possessed by his longing to be a steamboatman, he had decided once that he would voyage across the South Atlantic and enter Brazil and explore the headwaters of that other great river, the Amazon.

He had never reached the Amazon, but he had become a steamboatman. He had been one of the finest pilots of the high-wheeled packets on the Mississippi. He had worn handmade polished boots and a silver watchchain and a coat that made him look like a duke.

He had earned his glory, too. Under the hard, stern eyes of Mr. Bixby, the veteran of a thousand voyages, he had learned the shape of that great river in all the changing lights, all the changing weathers which made it a different river from night to night, from day to day. He had come as close to being a master of the river as any man could come. No man ever mastered the Mississippi, once and for all.

The mountains of Nevada, here around him, held dangers for a single traveler. There were mountain lions and wandering Indians and gold hunters who had become bandits, men who had committed murders and were ready to murder again. He had his pistol in his belt and he was prepared to use it to defend his life, if he had to.

But he had never felt, here in the mountains, the terror that had gripped him in the pilot's cabin of a steamboat thundering down the Mississippi through a night of fog and rain. If his judgment went wrong, up in the high cabin, the ship might ram another vessel and sink with its crowd of passengers. Or it might smash suddenly through a scow or a coal boat, or run aground, or crash against a reef.

In the days when he was a pilot, he had nothing to guide him except his memory and his feeling of the ship under him, his knowledge of the shifting channels, his instinctive sense of places to avoid. In those days there were no lighthouses or permanent buoy lights anywhere along the three or four thousand miles of twisting river. He had to go by his guts and his brains.

As he walked on in the wilderness, Sam Clemens tilted his head and stared at the black sky filled with the silver pepper of the stars. He remembered the swirling eddies, the gleaming currents rushing in the river under the stars on clear nights. The river was treacherous in starlight, deceptive in its gleaming ways.

Maybe that was why he had loved it so long, because it was just as changeable as he was, because it always held some surprise, some new turn to rouse the excitement of a restless man. Maybe if the Civil War hadn't broken out, he'd have remained on the river, he'd have become a pilot with as many legends as Mr. Bixby.

Walking slowly down the steep side of a hill, he shook his head. No, there wasn't much doubt he'd have left the river sooner or later. He had learned its shifts and moods too thoroughly, he had come to guess what they would be, and the river had lost its romance for him.

Its beauty and its poetry died away from him when he watched its ripples and its dark swirls with a pilot's eyes, wary of hidden snags, wary of sand bars, wary of all the trouble hidden under its shining surface. He got to feel like a man in a cage with a tiger. It was a handsome tiger, but he couldn't see it the way a painter might have seen it; he had to keep it from destroying him.

He'd never go back to the river, even if the war ended soon. He was a failure as a miner, as a timber cutter, as a prospector; but he couldn't leave the West. There were still other things he could do here.

The river was a big thing, but this country full of mountains was a bigger thing. Nevada was a place where he woke up in the morning with the sun blazing on him. Nevada was a place where he felt as though he could walk all night and all day and then jump ten feet straight in the air.

Here was a land enormously rich in gold, silver, copper, lead, coal, iron, quicksilver, marble, and granite. Here was a country where people of all kinds flocked to seek their fortunes — New Englanders, Scotsmen, Canadians, Chinese, Spaniards, poets, gamblers, sharpers, preachers, thieves, murderers, and desperadoes. Here was a land with room enough for them all.

He reached the crest of another high slope, and he halted for a moment, loosening the straps of his pack. The strange deep stillness of the desert spread far around him. Huge and heavy, immovable, unshakable, the mountains stood silent under the dazzling glitter of the stars.

Here was a country too vast for any man to comprehend. No matter how many people rushed into its valleys and hills, no matter how many huts and cabins were built, no matter how many towns sprang up, crowded with wagons and men, the land seemed lonely and empty. Its immensity could not be filled.

The desperate struggle for silver and gold, the bitter labor with picks and shovels, the dreams and despairs of miners and prospectors — his kind of men, the wild band to which he had belonged — dwindled down in his mind while he halted there, caught in the enormous silence of the Nevada night. The poor human race, squabbling over pieces of rock, seemed to him a race of crazy pygmies.

Then he had the feeling which came to him often — a feeling that had grown stronger in him year after year, and would grow stronger through his whole life. He had the feeling that this vast world, the stars and the mountains, the towns and the people, the desert and the hills, had no more enduring substance than a cloud or a dream.

And he himself, with his pack on his back, his gun in his belt, his bearded face, his heavy boots, his memories of his childhood days in Hannibal, his glories as a pilot on a great steamer whistling on the river, his failures as a miner in these hills, might be only a part of some Sleeper's imagination, a restless wandering figure in an Almighty Thinker's changing mind.

He kicked a rock with his right boot and saw it go tumbling down the side of the hill, dust spurting up where it rolled along. When his boot struck the rock, he felt a jolt in his foot, and that seemed real to him. The world was there, the world was solid; this wilderness around him was a true wilderness, full of danger.

But in his dreams he had felt things as sharply as that rock had felt against his boot. He had seen people and animals moving in his dreams. He had been happy, he had been sad, he had been afraid — and when he awakened he found that the things which had frightened him, saddened him, or made him joyful were not real — they were just shadows hurrying through his brain.

Yet he knew he had to live as though the world he saw when his eyes were open had the reality of existence. He had to make a living. That meant he had to do something people would pay money for. That meant he had to sweat if he wanted more than beans and barley.

He had always wanted to keep the careless joys of boyhood. He had always wanted to play — to play that he was the leader of a band of blood brothers in the caves around Hannibal; to play that he was a prankish printer's devil, spattered with ink; to play that he was a big steamboatman, startling the world with a loud clear whistle; to play that he was a rugged lucky miner, with gold and silver jingling in his pockets.

Nobody could keep on playing forever. He had come around to admitting that. He hated to admit it, but he had to. He had used all the money he had saved from his pilot's wages, and he had borrowed too much from his brother Orion. He couldn't keep on taking Orion's money.

He walked on in the wilderness under the stars, facing toward the mountains.

After a long time, after he had been walking for hours in silence, weariness overwhelmed him. He took off his pack, unrolled his blankets, lay down on the arid ground, and wrapped the blankets around him. He went immediately to sleep.

He awoke in a shower of hot light from the sun, crawled from beneath his blankets, stretched his stiff legs. He found some dry sticks, made a fire, cooked a small breakfast.

Before he resumed his march he reached into his shirt pocket and took out a letter — the letter from Barstow, the business manager of the *Virginia City Enterprise,* offering him a job as a reporter for twenty-five dollars a week. The letters signed "Josh" he had sent to the *Enterprise,* describing in burlesque terms the life of miners at Esmeralda, had won Barstow's warm approval. The editors of the *Enterprise* were ready to take him on.

If he became a reporter, it meant the final abandonment of his hope to strike it rich. It meant he would be living by his wits, by his observation of people, by his way of writing what he saw. He wasn't sure he could make a living as a writer for a newspaper.

Being a reporter might not carry the excitement of mining, the feverish anticipation of wealth, the hunter's passion that throbbed in every man who swung a pick. But he was finished as a miner. He couldn't go back.

All day he walked through the hills, trying to decide what he should do, swinging first one way and then another, turning toward Esmeralda and then toward Virginia City. When night came again, he was exhausted. After scraping together a slight supper, he dropped into his blankets.

He couldn't sleep. He lay there through the night, looking at the stars, searching for an answer in the sky. He did not find one. He rose in the morning, tired and troubled, angry at himself, angry at the bleak desert, the desolate mountains.

There was a time to be a boy, and a time to be a man.

His time to be a boy was over. He'd rather stay a boy than anything in the world, if the world was real. But he was twenty-seven, and he had to go one way or another.

For a week he wandered in the wilderness, eating little, sleeping, and waking too soon, getting slow on his feet, feeling his pack get heavier and heavier. He hated the world. He hated the whole human race. He didn't want to go down into it and make a living.

But when he flung up his arms to shield his face from the sun in the burning days, and when he lay tired and sore under the stars at night, the question was before him: Sam Clemens, where are you? And the other questions clustered: Where are you headed? What are you going to do?

Those were questions that didn't bother a boy when he was playing. Those were questions that bothered a man with a full beard on his face, a pack on his back, a gun in his belt.

He moved in a long circle. Suddenly he found he was at Dan Twing's cabin, and Dan's dog was jumping on him, and Dan gave him a good welcome.

"We got some new diggings," Dan said. "Get your pick, Sam."

The sight of the pock-marked hills in Esmeralda, the sight of the sweating miners chopping at the torn ground struck him with a terrible force. He took his pick and he

went to the diggings once more; but at the end of one day he had decided to leave.

He picked up his pack again. He made the journey of a hundred and thirty miles from Aurora, in the Esmeralda area, to the wild boom town of Virginia City — the town roaring with riches from the Comstock Lode.

He trudged wearily along the wide main street of the noisy city — the roughest, hardest town in the West — and he was barely conscious of the shouting, the rattle and rumble of wagons, the sounds of loud music from the saloons. He passed Mexicans, Germans, Irishmen, Indians, Chinese, men from everywhere.

He found a frame building on C Street. A sign declared that here were the offices of the *Enterprise*. He wiped the desert dust from his beard and went in.

Denis McCarthy, one of the owners of the newspaper, saw him enter. McCarthy asked what he wanted.

"My name is Clemens," he said. "I've come to write for the paper."

Sam Clemens had made up his mind. The man who became Mark Twain, the great reporter of the West, the great writer of *Huckleberry Finn,* had reached the true beginning of his career.

6 | Nellie Bly's Race
Around the World

WITH BRISK STRIDES, a girl in a heavy plaid ulster mounted the gangplank of the Atlantic steamer *Augusta Victoria*. Her shoulders were straight; her way of walking was confident. She had a small kit-bag and a silk raincoat slung over one arm. A porter carried the rest of her luggage — a single black satchel.

It was the morning of November 14, 1889, and the girl in the plaid ulster was starting out on a race around the world, to try to break a speed record held by a phantom. At the top of the gangplank she paused and looked down at the dock below. Her pert young face glowed. Her green eyes sparkled.

"Nellie, is that all the baggage you have?" asked one of the friends who had come to the ship with her. He nodded toward the porter carrying the black satchel.

Nellie Bly touched the traveling cap which rested at a jaunty angle on her thick dark hair. She buttoned her ulster tightly around her neck, because the wind was cold.

"Yes," she said. "It holds everything I'll need."

"Nobody else would try to do this," said her friend, shaking his head.

She laughed. "I hope not. I hope nobody follows me."

The ship's whistle gave a warning cry. Her friends crowded around her. They spoke together. "Good-by, Nellie. Keep up your courage. Good luck, girl."

She was twenty-two, and she believed she could do anything she wanted to do. As a reporter for the *New York World,* she had already won fame for her courage in exposing brutality in the treatment of insane women on Blackwells Island. She was eager for adventure, and ready to face the risks she might have to run.

Her friends hurried down to the dock. Nellie Bly stood at the rail alone, waving to them. The gangplank was hauled in. The steamer began to glide through the water toward the Atlantic. The whistle blew once more.

"See you here in January!" she called.

It was a bright and beautiful morning, but the wind whipped her coat around her. Suddenly she shivered. She wished for a moment that she had not decided to take the trip in midwinter. She had chosen a route around the earth north of the equator, and she was sure to hit storms and rough weather in many places.

If she had the best of luck, she would make the great circle in seventy-five days. That was her goal. She had to do better than the imaginary Mr. Phileas Fogg, the hero

of Jules Verne's novel *Around the World in Eighty Days.*
She had promised Mr. Pulitzer she would do it.

As she stood there on the ship, looking at the cannon
on the Battery, she remembered how the idea had come
to her at three o'clock in the morning, after a night
without sleep. She had gone to a steamship company's
office the next day, studied timetables, reached the con-
clusion that it could be done.

Then she had argued with Joseph Pulitzer, publisher
of the *New York World*. He told her immediately that
the *World* had already considered the possibility of sending a reporter around the globe and had dropped the
notion.

"I'm going," she had said, slapping his desk. "You can't
stop me."

Pulitzer had snorted. "If I send anybody, it will be a
man. You haven't thought of the dangers a girl would
face."

"Oh, I have," she had said. "And I'm going. If you don't
send me, I'll go for another paper. And I'll go faster than
any man you send."

Finally Pulitzer had given in. Now she was on the first
stage of the journey. Now she had to prove how much
nerve she had. Now she had to demonstrate to the whole
world that an American girl could travel alone, and travel
faster than any man.

She glanced at the sailors on the ship around her. They seemed to be grim and surly. They gave her quick, hard stares.

She felt the full realization of what it took to go this way, to be completely dependent on her own wits and her own courage for survival.

She thought of the friend who had offered her a small revolver, saying, "You'll need this as much as your passport, Nellie." She had been tempted, but the little gun had looked too wicked, too deadly. She had refused it, answering, "I won't need it, I believe the world will greet me as I greet it."

One of the ship's officers came up to her. "Miss Bly, we want to welcome you aboard the *Augusta Victoria.*"

Her brief panic was over. "Thank you," she said, smiling. "Are we going as fast as we can?"

The officer grinned. "We're just getting under way. We're going to get you to London in a week. That's as fast as we can make it."

When the ship moved from the shelter of New York Harbor into the open sea, it began to roll. The officer, standing beside her, expressed the hope that she did not suffer from seasickness.

"This time of year we're bound to run into heavy seas," he said.

The girl felt the deck quaking and shifting beneath

her. Abruptly she turned and ran alongside the rail to a point far from him. She leaned far over.

Another passenger, passing her, said in a clear voice, "And that's the girl who's going around the world!"

She straightened her shoulders and left the deck. In her cabin she unpacked the few things she had placed in the black satchel — three veils, an extra dress, a pair of slippers, toilet articles, an inkstand, pens, pencils and paper, pins, needles and thread, a dressing gown, a flask and drinking cup, underwear, handkerchiefs, and a jar of cold cream for her face. She tried to forget the shaking and swaying of the ship.

The storms she encountered on the Atlantic did not weaken her determination. Gradually she became a sturdy passenger, able to go on deck in any kind of weather. The people on the ship did not think she had a chance of getting around the earth in fewer than eleven weeks, but they were friendly and kind to her.

In the middle of the night of November 21, the *Augusta Victoria* reached Southampton. A young correspondent for the *World*, notified by cable of her expected arrival, met her with a tugboat and took her swiftly to the dock.

"You've missed the regular train to London," he said. "Unless they make up a special train to carry mail, you'll miss your connection with the channel boat. You'll be late getting to Paris."

[75]

"I'm counting on my luck," said Nellie Bly.

Her luck held. There were mountains of mail, and the railroad dispatchers ordered the formation of a special train. A passenger coach was attached to it, and Nellie got to London.

In France she went without sleep to visit Jules Verne at at his home in Amiens. He wished her a happy journey, but declared with a twinkle in his eyes that he did not believe she would really make a faster trip than his Mr. Fogg.

She rode in an express train through a tunnel under the Alps, down through Italy to Brindisi. There she caught a steamer bound for Suez. She reached the entrance to the canal on November 27, exactly on schedule.

"Mr. Verne is wrong," she exulted to another traveler. "I am going to beat Mr. Fogg's record without any trouble."

Then came one of the most frustrating experiences of her long journey. The ship could go only six miles an hour through the Suez Canal, because any higher speeds created waves which damaged the canal banks. So Nellie had to pace the deck under a scorching sun, watching the Egyptians running alongside the vessel begging for money.

The passengers threw coins over the rail, but the money fell in the sand and the beggars could not seem to find it. They kept pursuing the ship, filling the air with their mournful cries.

She was glad when the ship finally left the canal and steamed to the beautiful island of Ceylon. She was disheartened by the news which greeted her at Colombo: she would have to wait five days for a ship to take her on to Singapore.

Those were the longest five days of her life. She rode in rickshaws all over the island; she explored the exotic gardens of Kandy; she visited the giant temples of Colombo. But all the while she was haunted by the passing of time. Her dream of returning to New York in triumph began to fade.

At last the vessel she had been seeking came into the harbor. She found the captain and the officers congenial and helpful. They assured her they would help her make up the time she had lost.

In Singapore she was given a little monkey, a clever and amusing little beast which relieved her loneliness and kept her smiling. Her friends on the ship had kept their promise to aid her, and the vessel had arrived December 18, putting her again on the schedule she had planned.

On the way from Singapore to Hong Kong, the ship struck a monsoon in the China Sea. Tremendous waves battered its sides. Water poured over the decks, broke the windows, hurled passengers into their cabins.

One night Nellie Bly awoke to the sound of lapping water. She looked down from her berth and saw the sea tossing near her. Waves were breaking in her cabin. The ship was groaning; the wind was howling.

She thought the vessel was going down. It was a terrible ending to face. It was hard to abandon her hopes, to realize that her luck was gone. She lay quietly in her berth, determined not to weep, determined not to be a panicky woman.

She had fought for a place in the world of men, and she had won it. She had to take the risks that went with it, without crying, without pleading for any special mercy.

In the next cabin, men were bailing out water frantically, cursing and shouting. The girl sat up, staring at the dark sea just below her, and she knew that she could not fight the sea. She knew that if she sprang down into it, she would be swept away.

The ship's engines kept throbbing and throbbing. The ship kept plunging forward, heading through the storm. And gradually the ship righted itself; gradually the water receded from Nellie Bly's cabin.

When the morning light came, the sea was subsiding. But it was still rough, still strong. When the girl went on deck, a wave threw her from one side of the ship to the other. She seized an iron rail and clung to it. Another wave swept her to the other side of the vessel, and again she caught a rail at the last moment.

She had a fierce determination to live. She would not let the sea take her.

And in spite of the storm, the ship made good time. She arrived in Hong Kong two days ahead of her schedule. But there she was subjected to another damaging delay.

Yet her luck did not fail her. She got aboard the *Oceanic,* the finest and fastest liner plying between Hong Kong and San Francisco. She discovered that the officers knew about her race.

"We'll see you through, Nellie," said Chief Engineer Allen of the *Oceanic*. "We'll get you to the States. From there on you'll have a breeze."

Nellie Bly laughed. "I know I'll make it now."

She celebrated New Year's Eve on the *Oceanic* in the midst of another storm. But the ship was seaworthy and she was not afraid. She had come as close to death as she could get. She was ready to swim the Pacific if she had to.

In Japan she found a country and a people full of enchantment, grace, and beauty. The minute she came into Yokohama, she thought she had found the Garden of Eden.

"The Japanese are the cleanest people on earth," she wrote home. "They are the most happy and the most cheerful people I have seen. They are graceful and good-natured."

She went to the shrines of the Japanese gods. She was interviewed by Japanese reporters with courtesy and friendship. She was delighted by the dancing of the geisha girls, the love of painting and poetry shown by the people, the warm hospitality she received everywhere.

When she left Japan, she vowed she would return soon. She did not want to leave, but time was pressing upon her. She could not give up the race she had begun, the race against time and a phantom.

As the *Oceanic* pulled away from the shores of Japan, Chief Engineer Allen took her to the engine room and showed her the sign he had painted above the engines:

FOR NELLIE BLY
WE'LL WIN OR DIE.

"We set a record for a Pacific crossing on our last trip," said Allen. "This time we'll set a new record — for you, Nellie."

"If I fail, I'll never return to New York," she said.

"You won't fail."

For the first three days, the sea was smooth and the *Oceanic* moved at top speed. On the third day, the ship was a hundred and ten miles ahead of its previous crossing, which had broken all records.

Head winds hit the ship on that third day. The winds blew without ceasing for the next five days. The *Oceanic* fell a full day behind her schedule.

Nellie went to the captain's cabin. The chief engineer and the purser were there, looking gloomy. Only the captain seemed calm and hopeful.

"Isn't there anything to be done?" she begged. "I'd rather go in dead and successful than alive and behind time."

"Don't talk that way, child," Allen said. "I would do anything for you in my power. I have worked the engines as they never were worked before."

"I'll bet every cent I have in the bank that you'll be in New York before you're due," the captain said. "Just take my word for it, you'll be in New York at least three days ahead of time."

She was encouraged for a while, but the winds did not abate and she was soon in despair again. Rumors ran through the ship that monkeys brought bad luck, and it was suggested to the girl that she should permit the sailors to take the pet monkey she had received in Singapore and toss it overboard.

She believed in her luck, but she did not swallow that superstition. She would not consent to any such cruel treatment for the little monkey.

The night before the ship was due to dock in San

Francisco, the purser came rushing to her, his face pale.

"My God, the bill of health was left behind in Yokohama," the purser shouted.

"What does that mean?" the girl demanded.

"It means no one will be permitted to land until the next ship arrives from Japan. That will be two weeks."

Nellie cried, "I would cut my throat, for I could not live and endure it. Two weeks!" She caught her breath. "Please search for it. Please try to find that bill of health."

He made another search and finally came upon it lodged in a drawer in a desk belonging to the ship's doctor. Nellie Bly breathed hope again.

But when the ship at last reached San Francisco, newspapers brought aboard by revenue inspectors contained headlines saying that heavy snows had halted rail traffic to the East for the past week. The girl was shaken by this news. Her luck seemed to have forsaken her.

Then she found a special train waiting for her — a train consisting of a sleeping car, the *San Lorenzo,* and a huge engine, the *Queen*, one of the fastest locomotives on the Southern Pacific line. She learned that a southern route had been opened, the tracks had been cleared, the train was ready to go.

With the little monkey in her arms, she got aboard. The train went whistling down through the San Joaquin Valley at seventy miles an hour.

"I'm going to make it," she said joyfully. "I'm going to make it now."

When the train stopped at Fresno, the whole town turned out to greet her. Men asked her about her sunburned nose, the delays she had encountered, the number of miles she had gone. Women looked at her travel-worn dress, her cloak and cap, her single black satchel, the monkey she carried.

Her luck returned just when she needed it. The train went safely across a bridge which collapsed immediately after the locomotive and sleeping car had passed over it. In Arizona, a fresh engine was attached to the car. The other locomotive had just switched to another track when it lost a wheel.

No accidents delayed her any longer, no troubles plagued her on the last stage of her journey. As she crossed the country, she found that people everywhere had been reading reports of her race against time.

Ten thousand people cheered her in Topeka. "Come out here and we'll elect you governor," a Kansan shouted.

In Chicago she received a wild reception at the Press Club and the Board of Trade. She was given a cable from Jules Verne, saluting her for a magnificent achievement.

The depot in Columbus, Ohio, was swarming with people. They roared their applause. "Hurrah for Nellie Bly! You'll do it, Nellie, you'll do it!"

Many newspapermen and personal friends crowded aboard the train in Philadelphia. She was advised to jump to the platform in Jersey City the moment the train stopped. That would be her official arrival time — the moment her feet landed in Jersey City.

As the train came chugging into the New Jersey terminal, the crowd there broke through the lines of policemen assigned to guard the girl. Flowers were thrown at the train. In the uproar the delegation of officials there to greet Nellie could not make themselves heard.

The girl leaped from the platform. Stop watches registered the exact time. Cannons boomed from the Battery. A great shout went up to the sky.

Nellie Bly had made the trip around the world in seventy-two days, six hours, and eleven minutes. And she had become the best-known woman reporter in the world.

She took off her traveling cap and waved it to the crowd. She wanted to yell, too, because the long journey was over — because she was home.

7 | Stephen Crane Hunts the Truth about Courage

Wʜᴇɴ ʜᴇ ᴡᴀѕ seven or eight years old, Stephen used buttons from his mother's sewing kit as soldiers, lining up the ranks, sending his troops on fast marches across the carpet. When he was ten or eleven, he fought over the battles of Antietam and Chancellorsville, Bull Run and Chickamauga, the siege of Vicksburg, the struggle at Cold Harbor. Veterans of the long fighting between the North and the South were strong and swaggering in the streets of the town where he lived, and some of them liked to tell what they did or thought they did when the bullets sang around them. He listened, and sometimes he felt as though he had been there, too.

Stephen Crane was a skinny boy, easily winded, frail of face, but full of energy, full of nerve. All he knew about war was that it was riddled with danger; the veterans said so. A soldier with courage was a good soldier. Whether on the winning side or among the losers, a brave man had to be admired.

When he went to school in Asbury Park in New

Jersey, and later at the Hudson River Institute in the Catskills, he liked two things more than others: baseball and history. History seemed to him a chronicle of war, of victories and defeats, of courage and cowardice. It seemed to him, with the guns of the Civil War echoing in the stories he had heard, that men could not live without war, without proving that they were brave.

He was not too sure that he had any bravery in him. He did not enjoy the blows he exchanged with the other boys he knew; he did not love fighting for the sake of fighting. It was a way of trying out his courage and the courage of his friends.

He was not sure that any of the boys were any braver than he was. Some of them appeared to be very brave, and yet they had never been in an actual war. He believed it took a real war to test a boy or a man.

He did not know whether he would have a chance to be in a war. He had a feeling that he would not live very long. He did not think he would last until he was thirty-five. He had to hurry; he had to do something in a hurry. He had to show that Stephen Crane was different from any other man who ever lived; as brave as the bravest, but apart from all others.

When he was fifteen, he got the idea that he would like to be a professional ball player. Played right, a game of baseball was a hard fight. It took endurance; it called for daring. Each game was a battle. If there wasn't going to be another real war, baseball might give him the trial, the ordeal, he wanted.

He was a stubborn catcher, a swift shortstop, a far-ranging outfielder. He liked to catch. Slight as he was, with his long thin hands he could take the hottest pitches thrown at him. He could hit, too. When his turn came at bat, he stepped to the plate, gathered his strength, and lashed at the ball.

But his father had been a minister, and his mother didn't think baseball was a serious occupation. His older brother Will said he had to go to college before he decided what he wanted to do.

So he went to the Hudson River Institute, which had absorbed Claverack College and offered military training as well as academic courses. He was good on the drill field. In his years there, he became a captain of cadets, a leader on the baseball diamond, a student who questioned everybody and everything.

During the summer months he rode a bicycle along the shores of New Jersey, hunting items for his brother Townley, who had a news agency at Asbury Park. He tried writing feature articles, and found that writing could challenge him as much as baseball. He began to think about being a newspaperman.

He read the books he wanted to read and neglected the

books his teachers asked him to study, so he didn't make much progress as a student in the Hudson River Institute. He shifted to Lafayette College in Easton, Pennsylvania, and suffered from the brutal hazing then inflicted on new members.

He hated the humiliation to which he was subjected. When a group of sophomores broke into his room one night, he stood in a corner with a revolver in his hand. He was not ready to submit to any more physical punishment. One sophomore who was there said later, "His usual sallow complexion seemed to me a ghastly green."

That was an ordeal he could not endure. That was one time when his courage failed him. The sophomores walked out, and Crane stayed on for a while at the college, but he soon moved on to Syracuse University. He started the winter term there in January, 1891, living most of the time in the Delta Upsilon house, playing poker with his fraternity brothers, reading, smoking, and writing pieces for the *Detroit Free Press* and the Syracuse papers.

When summer came, he returned to Asbury Park, to work for Townley as a reporter, to lie on the beach, to dream and talk, to watch the ocean rolling upon the shore. He did not go back to Syracuse again. His college days were over.

He was still looking for a war, for a full test of his nerve, for the chance to find out whether he belonged among the brave. He tried to forget the fear which had seized him when the hazers broke into his room at Lafayette. Any man might give way once to the fear which trembled in every man somewhere.

That fall he found a game which seemed closer to the actual clash of war than baseball had ever been — the rough combat without weapons, the fierce game called football. In Lakeview, New Jersey, where he lived for a while with his brother Edmund, he formed the town's first football team. He coached it, he drilled it, he sent the two lines of men smashing together in hot scrimmages.

Weighing only one hundred and twenty pounds, Crane was too thin and too fragile to be a topflight gridiron man. The only position he could attempt to play was that of quarterback. Even then, he got knocked off his feet and hurled aside.

But he loved it. His heart leaped with excitement when the two lines grappled, the back men ran around the flanks, the guards tackled and toppled the runners. He saw in it the strategy of war, the surprises, the confusion, the demands of endurance, the swirling struggle of men trying to find the limits of their utmost strength.

Just before Christmas of that year, his mother died. He moved into New York, to try his own strength against the city, to take his own place in the army of hopeful young men always pouring into it, always trying to capture its towers. He was going to be a reporter — the best reporter New York had ever seen.

He got assignments from the *Herald,* writing about politics, police courts, accidents, the strife and turmoil of the swarming streets. But he didn't care about the details of names and addresses, all the details which editors valued.

He was Stephen Crane. He had his own way of writing, his own way of covering a story, his own way of looking at everything. Editors chopped his stories, insisted on what they called facts, harassed him and shouted at him. Finally the *Herald* fired him.

He found himself almost penniless, without a job, drifting in the streets. His brothers were willing to help him; his friends were ready to lend him money; and sometimes when he was desperate he took their help. He borrowed from other newspapermen, actors, young doctors he had met at the city hospitals. But he had no foothold in the city.

Now he realized he was in a battle, a clawing struggle o gain a place for himself. He slept on couches in the partments of friends. He went hungry for days. He spent nights in Bowery flophouses.

He hunted for the truth about this war — the war in the city, in which many were wounded and many were lost forever. He tramped in a snowstorm with beaten men waiting for a soup kitchen to open. He watched them shambling aimlessly beneath the iron pillars of the elevated railroads. He listened to their muttering talk, he heard the brief and bitter histories of their lives.

And while he never abandoned his compassion for them — he had compassion for nearly every living thing in the world — he made up his mind about them. They were permanently beaten because they had lost the will to fight. Any man could be kicked down, just as men in a football team could be smashed to earth. But men with courage never lay in the mud; they got to their feet again.

That was the way it seemed to him. That was the savage truth which hit him in the eyes and in the heart.

These were his hard and hungry years. Few editors would print his stories. He had to publish his novel *Maggie* himself. When it was published, he could not get people to buy it. He was ignored and rejected in a hundred ways.

He swore he would not go down. And he didn't. He had the spark of victory in him. He would not stay in the Bowery swamp of despair. He would not become one of the men who shuffled aimlessly along an empty street.

For a long time he had been thinking of a book about war, a simple story which would reveal what happened in the mind and heart of a young man plunged into the furnace of combat. He had done some work on this story in college. Now he tried it again; he put into it all his own doubts, his own arguments, his own inner conflicts, all the things that he imagined about the feelings of a man first faced with the necessity of killing or being killed.

He had heard the veterans talking of the Civil War. He had gone through book after book which had described the sights and sounds of carnage. Yet those books did not tell how the men felt as they fought. The books did not try to get into the mind of a young soldier, to witness the growth of fear and the rise of courage. His book would do that.

Crane stayed for months in a studio on East Twenty-third Street rented by R. G. Vosburgh, an illustrator, and two other artists. He worked at night, from midnight until four or five in the morning. He told his friends about the men in the story, the development of the battle, the bravery and then the flight of Henry Fleming, the young private, and Fleming's return to the struggle, Fleming's high courage.

Perhaps Fleming's breakdown and headlong flight in the early hours of battle represented Crane's breakdown when he stood that night in his room in the fraternity house and saw the sophomores battering through the door. Perhaps Fleming's recovery of nerve was linked to Crane's own recovery, Crane's endurance through years of trial.

When the book was finished, Crane took it to Hamlin Garland, who had achieved some fame as a writer and had shown him some friendliness. Garland was astounded, knowing that Crane had never been in the army and had never seen a war with guns. Yet this book gave an over-powering feeling of truth.

Garland asked how he knew about war. Pale and hollow-eyed, Crane grinned. He declared he had gained his knowledge on the football field. Describing this reply, Garland wrote later that Crane had told him, "The psychology is the same. The opposite team is an enemy tribe."

Impressed by its power, Garland tried to get the book published. He showed it to S. S. McClure, who had just started a popular monthly magazine. McClure gave every sign of enthusiasm — so much, in fact, that Crane informed a friend, "I have just sold another book" — but McClure hesitated and delayed, and at last did not buy it after all.

Then Irving Bacheller, a young man who was running the *Philadelphia Press* syndicate, agreed to print it as a serial in condensed form. In this form, reduced from twenty-four chapters to sixteen, it appeared in the *Press* and many other newspapers early in December, 1894.

Few books stir newspapermen, but Crane's did. When he visited the *Press* in Philadelphia, he was greeted by editors, reporters, proofreaders, compositors, who gathered around him to shake hands. They felt he had painted a true picture of a boy's fear and triumph in the midst of battle. He had shown what war was like.

When the book was published in England as well as in America, Crane leaped to fame. The youth who had wanted to be a baseball player was hailed as one of America's great writers. George Wyndham, one of England's leading critics, declared, "Mr. Crane's picture of war is more complete than Tolstoi's, more true than Zola's."

People were shocked when they found that *The Red Badge of Courage,* as the book was titled, had been written by a young man in his early twenties who had never seen a battle. It was hard for the critics to believe that Crane, the realistic reporter of war, had drawn entirely upon his imagination and his knowledge of football scrimmages.

Then came an actual war — the conflict between Greece and Turkey in 1897. Crane sought a job as a correspondent to cover the fighting, and was hired by the *New York Journal*. In London, on his way to Greece, he told William Heinemann, the publisher, that he'd written so much about war it was high time he saw a little fighting. In a letter to a friend, he said, "I am going to

Greece for the *Journal,* and if the *Red Badge* is not all right I shall sell out my claim to literature and take up orange growing."

He had to know. He had to see for himself. He had to find out whether the old veterans knew what they were talking about. He had to learn what happened to a man when the first shell went screaming over his head.

And he was looking for the moment when he could put himself to the final test. He was rushing, he was hurrying to see and know all he could. He did not have much time. He was still sure he would not live very long.

In Greece he was watched by the other correspondents. He was famous. He had been labeled a great novelist, a superb writer. But he had to prove that he himself had the courage he held up to the world as a man's finest quality.

John Bass, chief of the *Journal* correspondents in Greece, cabled to the Hearst newspapers a description of how Crane acted on the battlefield. Bass reported, "Amid the singing bullets and smashing shells, the novelist stopped, picked up a fat, waddling puppy and immediately christened it Velestino, the Journal Dog." Circled by danger, Crane had shown his quick compassion.

Crane won the respect, even the admiration, of the other reporters for his cool ability to gather news and to turn out stories under fire. The war was short; the

Greeks collasped in a few weeks under the superior force of the Turkish army. Crane went back to England.

"The *Red Badge* is all right," he said.

He had demonstrated his personal bravery. And the soldiers in Greece had behaved as the soldiers had behaved in his book. His imagination had caught the truth about men at war.

But his search was not over. He had not found the moment he sought — the moment of heroism. Something in him still demanded a greater ordeal than any he had undergone.

He attained it in Cuba, a year later, as a correspondent for the *New York World,* toiling up San Juan Hill with the American forces fighting to liberate the Cubans from Spanish rule. He made the supreme gesture — not of bravado, not as a display of nerve, but a gesture defying the powers of destruction and death.

On the crest of a ridge before San Juan, Stephen Crane rose to his feet and stood facing the fire of the Spaniards in a light raincoat that made him a perfect target.

There were some in the American ranks who thought he was delirious. He had been ill for weeks. He had been suffering from fevers. At times he had been exhausted and incoherent.

But there he stood, facing the fire of the enemy. Perhaps when he had been a small boy, using his mother's sewing buttons as soldiers, he had dreamed of such a moment. Bullets fell all around him, but he stood like someone dreaming, a man determined to face the whole snarling threat of violent agony, a man who wanted to draw all the menace of the battle upon himself.

Bullets filled the air, but did not harm him. Colonel Leonard Wood, huddled in a shell hole with Richard Harding Davis, bellowed at him to get down. He paid no attention.

Then Davis, who had already earned a reputation as one of the bravest reporters of his time, yelled at Crane. Crane fell to the grass and crawled behind a mound of earth, the light coat dragging behind him.

In a few minutes Crane got on his knees and then stood up again, gazing toward the enemy and the air glittering with gunfire.

Davis shouted, "Colonel Wood and I are not impressed by your courage, Crane."

Reporting this later, Davis said, "He blushed scarlet before he lay down."

When Colonel Wood moved away, Crane rose again. Perhaps he was striving to live out the dream of courage he had carried in him as a boy. He was in a real war and real death was all around him, but his dream was stronger — the dream of glory always alive in the heart of a boy.

Davis sprang to his feet, hurdled over some soldiers,

and slammed Crane to the earth. Two bullets whined at that instant, one knocking off Davis's hat, one clipping a piece from his binocular case.

But the bullets did not touch Stephen Crane. He did not get what he seemed to seek: to know what it was like to be wounded, to be badly wounded, perhaps to die in battle. He had hunted the truth about courage to its very limits, and he could go no farther.

He died young, as he had known he would — at the age of twenty-eight, two years after the fighting at San Juan — but not in battle.

8 | The Capture and Escape of Winston Churchill

THE British armored train moved slowly along a rail line in South Africa on a cloudy November day in 1899. Soldiers crouched low in the front cars, and sailors on a flatcar manned a naval gun. In the locomotive cab, close to the engineer, rode a young man with many freckles, red hair, and a bulldog jaw. He wore a correspondent's uniform and he was supposed to be a noncombatant, but he was armed and poised for the fray.

A month before, hostilities had begun between the British and the Boers of the Transvaal Republic. The Boers had given the Empire troops some stiff blows. The armored train had been sent on a scouting mission to learn the size of the gathering Boer forces.

The red-haired correspondent, Winston Churchill, knew he was headed for trouble, riding in that train. They had found plenty of Boers, and they had quickly decided to get back to the British base. But there were Boers across the rail line, cutting off the train's retreat.

When the engineer, a civilian, saw the Boers there, he

threw the locomotive into higher speed. The engine had three flatcars in front of it and two armored cars behind it. Two other cars were coupled to the tender, and three to the cowcatcher. As the train rumbled around a curve, the leading car struck some boulders which had been placed on the track.

The car toppled over with a clang, and the train came to a grinding halt. The rail line was blocked.

As Churchill leaped from the locomotive, he heard the scream of shells and the crackle of Boer rifles. With two field guns on the nearby hills and riflemen in position, the Boers began to hammer the train with a barrage of steel.

While the British troops in the armored cars returned the Boer fire and the naval gun hurled six-pound shells at the enemy, Churchill took charge of a group of soldiers and civilian railwaymen who struggled to get the over-turned car off the track. While the group sweated to move it, the engine rammed and pushed it.

Boer shells slammed into the train and the locomotive. Any instant one might hit the hot boiler. If it did, there would be a great explosion — and that would be the end of Churchill and the men around him. Many were wounded by shell fragments and the Boer marksmen; many fell to the earth.

For a brief time, Churchill felt the bitter touch of despair. Death seemed very close. Then the overturned car suddenly tilted, the engine groaned — and got through to the clear track. The wounded within reach were loaded onto the locomotive, the cowcatcher, the tender. As the engine began to grind forward, Churchill climbed aboard.

A shout came from the cars behind, which could not get through. Churchill turned and saw that one British soldier had tied a white handkerchief to a rifle. Lieutenant Frankland, an officer Churchill admired, was trying to rally the remaining troops to continue the fight. Churchill could not bear to see Englishmen fighting while he rode off.

He sprang from the engine, which had just entered a narrow ravine which protected it from the Boer shells. Walking toward him were two tall dark figures. They raised rifles, and bullets ripped the air, passing within a few inches of his head.

The English troops were being rounded up as prisoners. Churchill turned and scrambled along the railroad embankment. A bullet grazed his hand.

A Boer horseman came galloping toward him. He reached for the pistol he ordinarily carried, but could not find it. It had dropped off in the locomotive when he had jumped from the cab.

He was unarmed, encircled, outnumbered. Still, he hated to surrender. The thought flashed through his mind of what he had written, just two days before, in a dispatch to the *London Morning Post*: "There has been a great deal too much surrendering in this war, and I hope people who do so will not be encouraged."

But he did not want to die. He had much to live for. He had already decided that he would aim high in his career. If he lived, he intended to be one of the rulers of the Empire — the King's Prime Minister.

He raised his unwounded hand into the air. The men on the rail line below him stopped firing. The Boer on horseback accepted him as a prisoner.

With the other British captives from the train, he had to march for many miles to Pretoria, the capital city of the Transvaal. There he was put in the State Model School, which had been converted by the Boers into a military prison for British officers.

From the moment the gates closed behind him, he began to think of getting free again. He demanded to be released as a war correspondent, as a noncombatant, but the Boers knew too well that Winston Churchill could not be a noncombatant.

Night after night he watched the sentries pacing the walls under the glare of the prison lights. He discovered that there was one place on one wall where there seemed to be shadows, where the lights did not quite reach. There might be a chance of escaping over that wall.

Occasionally, he noticed, a sentry would leave a post and walk over to the next post for a cigarette and a talk with another sentry. He decided to take advantage of this behavior. He resolved to scale the wall in the shadowed place while a sentry's back was turned.

He related his plan to two officers — Captain Haldane, who had been in command of troops on the armored train, and a Lieutenant Brockie. They joined him in the scheme. They agreed to make the assault on the wall on the night of December 11.

The night came. Fortune was not favorable. The sentries seemed to be especially alert and did not give Churchill or his friends the slightest opportunity. They postponed the attempt until the next day.

When that night arrived, Churchill approached the wall alone. Something had delayed his friends. He was impatient, restless, determined to let nothing stop him. He did not wait for them too long.

He saw his chance. Two sentries got together and lit cigarettes. Creeping silently to the shadowed section of the wall, Churchill leaped for its top edge. He got his hands on it twice, and twice he was about to pull himself up when a sense of danger halted him.

The risk he ran was very great. The sentries were only fifteen yards apart. They were picked marksmen. If one of them turned and caught a glimpse of him, bullets

would rain on him. At that distance, he was almost certain
to be hit.

He was afraid and he had reasons to be afraid. He fought
his fear, there alone in the dark, and he overcame it. He
hurled himself at the wall a third time. He got on the
wide flat top of the barrier, drew a breath, rolled across
the wall, and dropped down into the garden of a house
on the other side of the prison.

The house was blazing with lights. Evidently the people
there were having a party. If one of them had glanced
toward the wall, his falling figure might have been seen.

Luckily, he had fallen behind a screen of bushes. There
was no alarm, not a sign that anyone had noticed him. He
lay there, panting, hoping that his friends would soon
make the leap and land beside him.

He waited in the bushes for an hour. People walked
along the graveled paths in the garden but did not see
him. Then he heard the voices of two British officers
coming through the prison wall behind him. He recognized Haldane's tone, and Brockie's. While one spoke and
laughed loudly, the other said, "We can't get out. It's
all up. Can you get back again?"

Go back? He'd never go back. He set his jaw. He made
the hard, stubborn decision — the kind of decision he
made many years later, when England stood alone, facing
Hitler's bombers. Churchill said, "I shall go on alone."

Now he felt that boldness was his only ally. He rose to his feet and strode through the garden, his head held high. He needed a miracle and he got a miracle. He was not discovered or challenged by anyone.

Humming a tune, he entered the street beyond the house. An entrance to the prison was just five yards away to his right. A Boer sentry guarded the gate. If the man recognized him, his fate was sealed.

Without breaking his stride, acting as though he might be a Boer burgher out for a stroll, Churchill went steadily along the street away from the prison. His shoulders were tense. His neck grew stiff. He expected a shot to be fired with each step he took.

The sentry apparently did not recognize him. Unscathed, young Churchill entered one of the principal streets of Pretoria. It was brightly lighted and crowded with Boer burghers.

Some days before, when his appeal for release as a war correspondent and "noncombatant" had been rejected, he had managed to "lose" his British campaign hat and had succeeded in buying a Boer sombrero from a prison guard. In the Boer hat, he was able to walk calmly through the crowds.

There were men from many countries in Pretoria then — Americans, Frenchmen, Germans, Russians who had enlisted in the Boer commando units — and there were many types of mixed uniforms. Few of the Boers gave any man a second glance.

Churchill made his way through Pretoria and got to the railroad tracks at the edge of the city. He knew that two rail lines left the Boer capital — one going to Pieter-maritzburg, and the other to the coast and Portuguese East Africa. If he could get into Portuguese territory, the Boers could not recapture him.

It was nearly midnight when he stood at the railroad tracks. He could not be sure which line would take him eastward to freedom. He resolved to take the first train he could board, knowing that he had to get as far from Pretoria as possible; once his escape had been discovered, he could not evade capture very long in the capital city.

A freight train came puffing slowly near him. He let the locomotive and the first few cars rattle past him; then he leaped into a car which seemed to be full of sacks. He found these were empty bags which had apparently con-tained coal. He burrowed down under them, concealing himself.

When dawn came, he saw that the train was moving east. He had no notion of where he was, but he knew he was going in the right direction. Elation filled him. He had new faith in his destiny.

He was sure that the news of his escape would spread quickly from Pretoria to the British forces in the field —

and then to England. He was also sure that the Boers would expend every ounce of energy they could devote to finding him and hauling him back to prison.

His capture had been a cause of rejoicing for the Boers, because he was a grandson of the Duke of Marlborough and because he was a leading correspondent for the *London Morning Post*. His escape would stir their relentless anger.

He could not stay on the freight train. It would stop soon, and when it stopped, it would be searched. The coal sacks would not hide him well enough. He had to take to the fields, and work his way around the Boer towns.

When the train slowed down on a hill, Churchill jumped from it, rolling into a thicket. He was unhurt. Brushing the dust from his clothes, he rose and went on. He headed in the same direction as the train, sticking close to the rail line, because he had no compass or map to guide him.

Seeking shelter from the glare of the sun, he entered a forest. Most of that day he walked in the woods. Above him came the sound of ungainly wings flapping. He glanced upward and found that he was being circled by a large vulture.

The sight of that bird of carrion made him realize the desperate nature of his plight. For food, he had only four slabs of chocolate which he had slipped into his clothes in the prison. Unless he found friendly people who would give him food, he might face the choice of surrendering again to the Boers or of being devoured by the vulture.

Churchill was a man of self-reliance, a man of action. He had seldom pleaded with God for aid. But in that forest, under the shadow of those menacing wings, he fell upon his knees and prayed that God would keep him from being that vulture's victim. He had resolved that he would not surrender to the Boers a second time.

He walked on, taking small bites of the chocolate as his hunger became intense. He came upon a narrow stream and drank from it. His legs and feet ached, and he wished that he had been able to stay aboard that freight train.

But his decision to leave the train had been a wise one. He knew this when he saw a railroad bridge in the distance and saw the Boer fighters around it. All the bridges and stations along the rail line would be closely watched. All the trains would be searched.

He decided to lie under cover by day and to walk ahead at night, when he might have a better chance of slipping through the Boer patrols. His description had undoubtedly been sent by telegraph to every Boer town.

Days and nights passed. He grew weaker. Chocolate was not enough to sustain a man struggling through the fields and forests of South Africa. His spirit was still strong, but his body was beginning to demand the satisfaction of its needs.

On the night when Churchill felt that he could not stumble on any longer, he saw the blaze of a fire in a clearing. He thought it might be a fire in the camp of some Kaffirs — African natives who had no love for the Boers and might be willing to assist an Englishman, if he could make them understand that he would reward them greatly for their aid. In any case, he had no alternative. He had to have food. He did not want to die.

As he came closer to the blaze, he paused for a moment. The light did not come from a campfire. It came from a house — one of several houses grouped around a mine shaft. He had stumbled into a mining settlement, not a Kaffir camp.

But he went on, because he had reached the end of his rope. He made up a story to tell the people in the house, a story that he hoped would convince them that they should not turn him over to the Boer armed forces. In his weary state, his head buzzed with confused plans.

He rapped on the door of the lighted house. A man called a sharp question in the Boer tongue. Churchill thought he was finished. All his determination to escape, all his struggling and suffering had not been enough.

The door was thrown open — and then Churchill found that it was not his destiny to be defeated. Some power had led him to the only house in the mining village inhabited by an Englishman.

He had knocked at the door of John Howard, the manager of the Transvaal Collieries, a mining engineer who had become a naturalized citizen of the Transvaal Republic but still had sympathies with England. Howard took Churchill in, fed him, and hid him at the bottom of the mine shaft while plans were made to get him across the border into Portuguese East Africa.

He was safe enough in the mine, and Howard kept him supplied with food, wine, and candles. But when the candles burned low, rats began to creep all around him. Sometimes, after he had fallen asleep and the candles had guttered out, he awoke and felt the rats crawling over his body.

Churchill endured the half darkness of the mine and the presence of the rats for several days with stoic strength. He had to depend upon Howard to choose the best moment for him to get over the border to freedom.

The day came when Howard had found the right way. A Mr. Burgener, a Dutchman who lived near the mine and was friendly to the British, was sending a large consignment of wool bales to Delagoa Bay in Portuguese territory. He agreed to have Churchill hidden among these bales.

The huge squares of wool were carefully arranged to provide enough space for a man to sit in a kind of cave, surrounded by wool walls. Churchill was taken hurriedly to the freight car and thrust into this hiding place. He was given a revolver, two roast chickens, some slices of meat, a melon, and three bottles of cold tea to sustain him on the rail journey to Lourenço Marques, the nearest Portuguese town.

After the freight train began to jolt along the tracks, Churchill made a small opening between two bales. Through this opening, which was near a crack in the side of the railroad car, he could see the countryside moving past him. Whenever the train halted at a station — and it halted often — he closed the opening and withdrew into his woolly cave.

When the train reached the border, it was stopped for eighteen hours while the Boer guards examined every car. Some of the guards jabbed at the mound of wool bales with their bayonets, but Churchill was not discovered.

At the end of that long search, the train began to move once more. Slowly it clicked and rattled over the track into Portuguese territory. Every second was a great moment of joy for Winston Churchill.

He was free, he was free!

He had to express his exultancy. He widened the opening he had made between the bales, thrust his revolver forward, and fired six shots into the air beyond the train. He laughed and shouted with delight.

When he got to Lourenço Marques, he went at once to

the British Consulate. Grimy and weather-beaten as he was, he received no recognition from a clerk there. But when he gave his name, the clerk ran into the inner office and the consul came dashing out, full of excitement.

Churchill was the man of the hour. English residents of Lourenço Marques, when they heard he was actually in the town, came to the consul's garden and formed a cordon of armed men around the house to protect him. There were many Boer sympathizers in the area, and Churchill was still in danger.

He went by boat to Durban, where he got a hero's welcome. The whole harbor was decorated with British flags. An admiral, a general, and the mayor of the city boarded his ship and shook his hand in fervent congratulations.

The story of his escape went round the world. His daring and his determination were applauded everywhere.

That same daring, that same determination, that same faith in his destiny made him a leader in two world wars and lifted him to the heights of glory as England's Prime Minister during the Battle of Britain in 1940. Steadfast and strong, Winston Churchill became a living symbol of England's strength.

9 | # Winifred Black Begs Help
for a Wrecked City

I‍t began to rain early in the morning, on that dark Saturday when the hurricane struck. The rain grew heavier, hour after hour. Whipped by the wind, waves from the Gulf of Mexico began to advance upon the city of Galveston, which had been built upon a sandy island at the very edge of the Gulf.

Days before, the United States Weather Bureau had given warnings of a powerful storm which had developed in the West Indies, southeast of San Domingo. The month of August had been fiercely hot and sultry, and some forecasters had predicted hurricanes with the advent of September and the approach of the autumn equinox.

The hurricane which had been detected off San Domingo had swirled first toward Florida, and then had turned west below Tampa and had slowly huffed across the Gulf of Mexico. On the morning of September 8, 1900, it swung straight inland toward Galveston. It pounced upon the city with all the might and ferocity of an enormous wild beast.

The rain suddenly fell in sheets which flailed into the sides of houses. Out of the Gulf reared a giant wave, a tidal wave of roaring, crashing water that swept through houses and buildings like a blade of steel.

People were trapped in the streets and whirled away screaming. Others were torn from their homes and tossed head first into the thundering wave. Hundreds were smashed by falling walls. Many more were buried beneath the timbers and bricks, the sticks and stones which once had been the city of Galveston.

The city had been proud of its fine harbor, the miles of docks, the ships which came to Galveston from all over the world. The harbor was wrecked. The smaller boats — launches, sloops, barges — were turned end over end and battered to pieces on the beach. Eight ocean liners were torn from their moorings and stranded in the bay.

In four hours the entire city had been covered by the waters. The wind, which had reached an initial velocity of one hundred miles an hour, was blowing a gale that howled and moaned through the wreckage. The rain still fell in blinding torrents.

All that afternoon and all that night the people of Galveston huddled in terror upon the tops of buildings and the roofs of the remaining houses which had not been completely demolished. All the lights of the city had gone out. The sky was veiled by black clouds.

Of the forty thousand people who lived in the city, six thousand had been killed. Many of the others had been injured. Many had lost their clothes and lay naked in the rain, weeping and praying. Many were afraid that everyone in the city might be doomed.

There seemed to be no way in which help could reach them. The bridges connecting Galveston Island with the Texas mainland had been destroyed. A train approaching the city when the storm struck had been lifted into the air and dashed in wreckage under the seething waters.

The Gulf was too stormy that night for rescuers in boats to get through. The people on the mainland were aware of the disaster. The nation was stunned by the horror but already moving to bring relief to the survivors.

During that night, the city was cut off. It was at the mercy of the wind and the waves — and the wind and the waves had no mercy for the living or the dead.

All through that night, the buildings on which the people huddled together were shaking and shivering. No one knew when the floors might crack and collapse. No one knew when the foundations might be ripped apart by the ravaging water.

When Sunday morning dawned, the people shuddered at the sights below them — the crumpled houses, the mud and slime everywhere, the bodies floating in the flood. It seemed then that Galveston had been crushed beyond any hope of reconstruction.

Some of the men who lay helplessly on the rooftops abandoned themselves to despair. But the women who had survived that night showed the stamina of Amazons. They tore pieces from their skirts to make bandages for the injured; they comforted the crying children; they soothed and encouraged the men.

And the waters began to retreat, slowly sinking back into the Gulf from which the destroying waves had come. Men climbed down into the choked streets and began to clear away the wreckage. Grocery stores were opened; food was distributed to the hungry.

But the city's plight was still desperate. The bridges were gone. The railroad tracks for miles inland had been twisted and made useless. The only way of getting food, clothing, and medicines to the city was to bring the supplies over water from Texas City, which was six miles across the bay.

On Monday the relief trains sent from other cities, carrying Red Cross workers, doctors, and nurses, were forced to turn back. Some of them steamed into Texas City, where there were men waiting to transfer their cargoes and relief workers to launches and sloops.

In one of the launches from Texas City, a few days after the disaster, rode the first reporter to reach Galveston from the outside world. The reporter was a tall, hand-some woman with red hair, a dazzling smile, and ruthless determination. She looked about her with bright, calm eyes, and she took in everything around her.

Winifred Black, star reporter for William Randolph Hearst, had been a chorus girl, a dancer, an actress. Then she had managed to persuade S. S. Chamberlain, the managing editor of the *San Francisco Examiner,* a Hearst paper, to give her a job — and she had done so well that Hearst had made her a roving correspondent.

She was a woman with deep emotions. And she had learned to write in a direct, clear style that carried her feelings into the hearts of others. Since many of her stories were about people in trouble, she often stirred sympathy and sorrow in her readers.

When the word came to New York that a tidal wave and storm had swept over Galveston, Hearst had told her to get to Texas on the fastest train she could catch. At Houston, she had boarded a relief train loaded with drugs, disinfectants, supplies of all kinds for the stricken city.

The train was driven by an engineer who had lost his family in the catastrophe, and it tore down through the Texas plain at a furious speed.

The supplies from the train were swiftly loaded aboard barges and launches bound for Galveston. But when Winifred Black walked to the Texas City wharf, she was halted by soldiers who stood in a line across the dock, their swords drawn.

Winifred Black pleaded with them. They stood with firm faces, barring her way. She smiled at them, tried to cajole them. They did not yield. She wept, and they ignored her.

Then one of the men who had been on the relief train from Houston helped her get on a small paddle-wheeled steamer which was bound for Galveston. As the steamer's paddles churned through the water, which now seemed smooth and pleasant, she saw a tower of fire shooting up toward the stars.

She thought some of the wrecked buildings in Galveston must be flaming on the horizon. The men on the steamer looked at her with faces of bitter grief, and one explained to her that the fire came from a funeral pyre. To keep pestilence from breaking out, the bodies of the flood victims had to be destroyed.

With her on the steamer was the United States Marshal of Southern Texas, a lean, bronzed man who asked her to stay close to him when they got to the smashed city. There were looters and vandals in the dark streets, and her life would be in peril unless she had the company of an armed man.

The scene she found in Galveston she made real to mil-

lions of Americans. She sent out a dispatch which painted the misery and the need of aid for Galveston in such vivid terms that she stirred a response from New York to San Francisco.

She wrote:

> We pulled up at a little wharf in the hush of the star-light; there were no lights anywhere in the city except a few scattered lamps shining from a few desolate, half-destroyed houses. We picked our way up the street. The ground was slimy with the debris of the sea. Great pools of water stood in the middle of the street.
>
> We climbed over wreckage and picked our way through heaps of rubbish. The terrible, sickening odor almost over-came us, and it was all that I could do to shut my teeth and get through the streets somehow. . . .
>
> We got to the hotel after some nightmare plodding through dim streets like a line of forlorn ghosts in a half-forgotten dream. At the hotel, a big, typical Southern hotel, with a dome and marble rotunda, the marble stained and patched with sea slime, the clerk told us that he had no rooms. We tried to impress him in some way, but he would not look up from his book, and all he said was "No room" over and over again like a man talking in his sleep.
>
> We hunted the housekeeper and found there was room, and plenty of it, only the clerk was so dazed that he did not know what he was doing. There was room, but no bedding, and no water, and no linen of any sort.

General McKibben, commander in charge of the Texas

division, was downstairs in the parlor reading dispatches, with an aide and an orderly or two at his elbow. He was horrified to see me.

"How in the world did you get here?" he said. "I would not let any women belonging to me come into this place of horror for all the money in America."

General McKibben told her that the number of dead and injured would be far higher than the first estimates had given. He said, "The people all over America are responding generously to our appeals for help, and I would like to impress it upon them that what we need now is money, money, money and disinfectants. Tell your people to send all the quicklime they can get through. What we must fight now is infection, and we must fight it quick and with determination or it will conquer us."

She wrote her dispatch hurriedly and gave it to a man who was leaving in a launch for Texas City. She begged him to take it to the Western Union office there and make certain that it went on the wire to New York at once.

Her dispatch was a cry for help. It ended:

The little parks are full of homeless people, the prairies around Galveston are dotted with little camp fires, where the homeless and destitute are trying to gather their scattered families together and find out who among them are dead and who are living. There are thousands and thousands of families in Galveston today without food or properties or a place to lay their heads.

It will take thousands and thousands of dollars to put them on their feet again. I believe that the people of America will see that money is not lacking. But, oh, in pity's name, in America's name, do not delay one single instant. Send this help quickly, or it will be too late.

The people in many cities and many states responded to her appeal, as they had responded earlier to the pleas of the leaders of Galveston, who had asked for assistance to prevent starvation and plague.

Carloads of food, medicines, disinfectants came from cities in every section of the country — St. Louis, Boston, Philadelphia, New Orleans, Cincinnati, Cleveland, Minneapolis, Denver, Pittsburgh, Kansas City, San Francisco, and other towns large and small.

The day after she had sent off her first dispatch, she was in her room at the hotel trying to get a little sleep after hours of walking through the ruined city. She was wakened by a series of telegrams, all announcing that four Hearst papers had relief trains on the way.

She was asked to have a hospital ready when the trains arrived with doctors, nurses, and full medical and surgical equipment.

"A hospital!" she exclaimed, crumpling the telegrams in her hands. "How can they expect me to set up a hospital in the midst of this wreckage?"

But she was an organizer, an administrator, an executive

as well as a reporter. William Randolph Hearst knew it. He had watched her organize reform movements and crusading groups to change the political corruption in American cities. He felt confident that she would have arrangements for a hospital by the time the trains arrived.

He was right. Winifred Black went to the chief of police, who had already become her friend, and got permission to take possession of a building which could be converted into a hospital. She got hold of eighty mattresses. She found men to clean the halls of the building.

She had everything organized when the trains came into the city over emergency bridges.

Hearst sent her sixty thousand dollars, earmarked for her personal account, for distribution to the homeless families in Galveston. She saw to it that the money got to those who were most urgently in need of aid. She formed a relief corps of her own and helped to raise another three hundred and fifty thousand dollars for the survivors of the flood.

Moved by the spectacle of suffering she found in Galveston, Winifred Black was not contented with the importance of her role as a reporter whose words stirred millions to open their hearts and their pocketbooks for the stricken people of the city. She could not be a spectator, a bystander in the ruins.

She had to do more — and she did it. When she made

people weep, she wept herself. When she asked people to give generously, she gave herself.

The people of Galveston had reason to be grateful for the deep feeling of pity and sorrow Winifred Black put into her dispatches from their devastated city. Other reporters came to the city and others wrote eloquently of Galveston's needs, but she had a way of stirring people's emotions which others lacked.

Newspapers in many cities, mayors, governors, church leaders, schoolteachers, people of all kinds and all walks of life were horrified and aroused to action by the Galveston disaster. Americans showed their generosity on a lavish scale, and people in other countries sent gifts for the use of Galveston families.

School children collected pennies and placed them in special Galveston funds. Workingmen gave some of their pay. Bankers and industrial leaders gave large sums.

Winifred Black was not solely responsible for the outpouring of assistance that came to Galveston. The response occurred immediately when people in the world heard about the extent of the catastrophe, the number of homeless families, the pitiful plight of starving children.

But Winifred Black told the story of the city's gallant fight to recover. Day after day she recorded the little incidents which were touching, the simple acts of kindness and good neighborliness which meant so much to men and women surrounded by grim destruction and haunted by recollections of tragedy.

There were some people who doubted that Galveston could continue to exist as a city. Winifred Black was not one of them. Her faith, her confidence, in the city's future was clear and bright in the stories she wrote.

She helped the people of the city to survive — and encouraged them to build a new city upon the wreckage of the old. The people of Galveston had plenty of courage and plenty of determination, and Winifred Black saw that they would not yield to despair.

From Galveston, she went on to cover other important stories. She became the best-known woman reporter in America. And because she was so successful in reaching people's hearts, another reporter later tagged her with an ironic name. He called her a "sob sister."

It was a title that people remembered. And because women reporters were generally given assignments that brought out the human side of the news — often the tragic events of life — the title of "sob sister" clung to them from then on.

10 | Seized as a Spy, Richard Harding Davis Faces a Court-martial in Belgium

---

Down a dusty road south of Brussels, in the third week of August, 1914, a Belgian taxicab careened at a rapid rate, carrying two American reporters who were trailing the German army. The gray legions of Kaiser Wilhelm had marched through Brussels and were thundering into France. The two Americans were determined to follow.

They had already been stopped once by German troops and ordered to return to Brussels. As neutral Americans, not yet involved in the war, they had certain privileges, but they had gone too far. Their passes, signed by General von Jarotsky, the German military governor of Brussels, simply granted them the right to move about the city and its "environs." They had gone beyond the boundaries of the zone in which they were permitted to travel.

The taller of the two men in the taxi — a handsome sunburned man with a calm, proud face — did not believe that the German army or any other army could set limits to his freedom. He was Richard Harding Davis, and his

[127]

name was a passport he considered good anywhere. He treated the whole earth as a place for him to roam where he pleased.

The younger man, Gerald Morgan, was worried. Morgan didn't like the grim faces of the Germans who had halted them a few miles back. He didn't think they would get off lightly if they were stopped again. And Morgan felt that the road on which they were traveling would not lead them to the big guns and the main battle they were seeking.

Finally Morgan ordered the cab to stop. The brakes screeched. Morgan said he thought it was time to turn back.

If they kept going, Morgan declared, they'd soon be collared and taken to Brussels under guard. They'd lose their passes. Then they wouldn't be able to get around to report anything. Besides, he was positive they would not find any fighting along this road. He was sure of it.

Davis listened, quietly and thoughtfully. He didn't attempt to argue. It was certainly possible that Morgan might be right. But he thought they should keep going — on foot if necessary.

If he had to go back, he wanted to be taken under guard. He had a job to do, and his idea of the job made him decided he had to run that danger. Maybe he was stubborn. Maybe he remembered the time in Manchuria when he had missed a battle because he had turned back a little too soon.

Morgan walked with him for a while. They marched alongside a German column which stretched for miles. Morgan kept urging him to turn back and Davis kept refusing. At last Morgan swung around toward Brussels.

Davis shrugged. Then he went on at a steady pace. He was calm and confident. He had been in five wars before this one — the Spanish war in Cuba, the struggle between the Greeks and the Turks, the Spanish-American fighting, the bitter conflict between the Boers and the British, and the war between the Russians and the Japanese. He had come through them all unharmed.

He was a straight, tall man with a soldier's bearing. He wore a brown suit made by an English tailor. As he strode along, he looked very much like an English officer in civilian clothes — although he did not realize it.

German troops came marching past him, moving at a quick pace. The Germans gave him searching glances, but they were in a hurry, driving toward the little village of Ath on the Dender River, where they aimed to strike the British army in a surprise flank attack. So they did not pause to question the strange man in the brown suit.

Shortly after noon, Davis found a pleasant stretch of grass near the road and decided to have lunch. He took some sandwiches from his haversack and sat down, his back against a tree. He was in greater danger than he had ever been in his life, and he was soon to become aware of it.

Just as he was biting into a sandwich, four German soldiers with pistols appeared before him. One weapon was pressed against his stomach. Their voices growled questions.

A moment before, he had felt comfortable — and bored. No shells had been exploding. No bullets had been whistling about him. He had been on the point of deciding that he would see no action on this road, as Morgan had predicted.

And all that time, the four Germans had been closing a circle around him.

He raised both hands in the air, one hand still holding the sandwich. He said his identification papers were in his coat.

One of the Germans understood English. That one ordered him to rise. Their pistols against his sides, he marched with them to the clump of trees a few hundred yards away, where they presented him to their colonel.

The colonel had just enjoyed a splendid lunch. That was fortunate for Davis.

Full of convivial spirits, the colonel gave a drink to the soldier who had captured Davis and then offered a drink to Davis. The colonel laughed, barely looked at his pass, and gave him permission to go as far as Enghien, two miles from the place where he had been halted.

But he had not gone many steps before he was stopped again, taken before another officer, and questioned. He was finally allowed to go on. He got to Enghien, and the Belgian burgomaster agreed to let him stay a night there.

The burgomaster handed him a permit but told him he did not really need it, saying, "As an American, you are free to stay here as long as you wish." Then the burgomaster winked, and Davis realized that the Belgian did not believe he was an American.

It was true that his credentials included a photograph of him in a military tunic — and the tunic was one he had designed himself, based on the officer's uniform of a British regiment he had admired in the Boer War. He did look British in that coat.

If the Belgian took him for a British officer, he must be considered a spy, because he was in civilian clothes, in territory occupied by the Germans, in the middle of a war. If the Belgian considered him so, the Germans must view him with deep suspicion. He knew what might happen to a man regarded as a spy, caught near the front.

That night he could not sleep. He heard the metallic clank and rattle of German artillery moving through the town; he heard the crash of the ironshod German boots hitting the Belgian cobblestones. All through the night, the gray-clad columns of the Kaiser's marching men went through Enghien.

At dawn he sat in his room in the town's hotel, thinking that he should turn back. He was running the risk of being executed as a spy. He might be shot against a wall, if the gray army decided that he might jeopardize its plans. Later, when he was listed among the missing, his death might be explained as an accident of battle.

He dressed slowly, and then went down into the street and began to follow the long gray lines of soldiers. That was his duty as a reporter. That was the way he saw it.

He passed a group of horsemen — apparently officers, judging by the elegance of their uniforms. One came after him, stopped him, ordered him to show his papers.

The mounted officer stared at the photograph of Davis in what seemed to be a British tunic. The officer frowned, tapped the papers, and called to a lieutenant and a sergeant.

"You'd better see our general," the officer snapped. "Get moving."

With the lieutenant and the sergeant as his guards, Davis found himself taking hard, quick strides, marching with the gray troops, who went thudding forward at a rapid pace, sweating but silent, stepping like mechanical men. Soldiers who fell were hauled to their feet and shoved again into the ranks.

Davis had always kept himself in fine physical condition. His health and stamina were needed then, because the Germans kept him striding forward for fully five hours. He rested only when the troops around him rested. He rose when they rose, and he marched in silence, as they did.

He broke one shoe on the Belgian cobblestones and the leather cut into his foot, but the Germans would not let him pause or slow his strides. Pain began to shoot through his leg, but he could not get out of their iron ranks.

He was almost at the end of his endurance when a large car, bearing on its sides the Kaiser's imperial eagle, came roaring down the road. The car stopped. A staff officer of high rank stepped from the automobile, spoke to the lieutenant, and ordered Davis to get into the huge gray machine.

Davis got in. The car took him swiftly to the division staff, which was having an elegant luncheon just off the road while the imperial troops marched past.

A tall, dark officer, in a uniform of light blue with silver braiding, came toward him. Davis was conscious of his broken shoe, the dust on his brown suit, and the fact that he was helpless in the hands of the German army. He knew that his life was at stake.

The officer did not indulge in any formalities. The accusations came at once.

"You are an English officer, not in uniform," said the German. "You have been taken inside our lines." A thin, muscular finger stabbed at Davis. "You know what that means."

Davis explained that he was a war correspondent. He said it was his job to follow armies. He tried a little flattery. "And yours is the best-looking army I ever saw."

The officer in the resplendent uniform bowed. "We thank you," he said. "But you have seen too much."

Davis answered, "I haven't seen anything that everybody in Brussels hasn't seen for three days."

The officer disagreed. The German thought Davis had seen enough to warrant an execution.

Davis later discovered that he had trailed a German army corps rushing to smash in the right flank of the British army. The Germans believed he knew what was going on. They were convinced that he would try to get information through their lines to the British forces.

"I am an American," he insisted. "I am Richard Harding Davis, the American correspondent. My passport proves it."

He suffered two severe shocks. The German officer pointed out that his passport had been given to him in London, as the document showed. The picture in the passport appeared to be the picture of a man in a British uniform. That seemed conclusive evidence that he was British, not American. And his second shock — and perhaps the worst shock of all — came when the German said he had never heard of an American correspondent named Richard Harding Davis.

Could it be possible that the officers of a division staff of the German army — men who were obviously well educated and well informed about the world — had never heard of an American reporter who had covered five earlier wars? Hadn't they read his novels, or heard of his plays, or seen a movie based on one of his books?

They insisted that they hadn't. They didn't seem to have the slightest realization that his execution as a spy — if they contemplated such action — would stir a storm of protest in the United States. They couldn't seem to realize that they would be incurring the wrath of American newspaper editors if they took such a step.

No matter how vigorously he protested, they continued to declare that they felt sure he was an Englishman. While they admired his daring in venturing into the midst of the German army, they weren't prepared to let him get away with it.

They laughed at him when he told them that the uniform he wore in the passport photograph had been based on one worn by the West African Field Force of the British army during the war against the Boers. They informed him that several English brigades now had the same type of uniform.

In addition to his inquisitor, Davis was surrounded by seven other elegant officers. All of them looked at him with smiles of amusement while he sputtered his protests. The handsome officer interrogating him suddenly demanded, "If you aren't a British officer, why are you wearing war ribbons in that photograph?"

Davis declared that he wore the ribbons to show the campaigns in which he had participated. "They prove that I am a correspondent," he said. "Only a correspondent could have been in wars in which his own country was not engaged."

The German officer came back with a quick reply: "You might get them if you were a military attaché."

After a time the German officers withdrew a little and began to discuss his case. He heard them shouting at one another. Evidently they were not in complete agreement. Some appeared to think he was a mad American; others appeared to be convinced that he was an English spy and should be shot immediately.

At last he was taken to a house in the Belgian town of Ligne, under guard. The court-martial had not felt confident enough of his British identity to have him shot, but he had not persuaded the officers that he was an

American. So he was placed in captivity until a definite decision could be reached.

Trying desperately to find a way out of his predicament, he asked a German major at the house to permit him to send a message to Brand Whitlock, the American ambassador in Brussels. The major seemed to credit his story, and went to consult superior officers.

But the major soon returned, shaking his head. Davis saw tears on the man's face. That indicated the German staff officers might be talking of sending him before a firing squad.

He had no time to lose. He had to think of something, and think fast.

An idea came to him. If he suggested that he be sent back to Brussels, how could the Germans suspect him of wanting to get through their lines to the British forces battling the Kaiser's army on the southern borders of Belgium?

Brussels was fifty miles away on the winding roads from the village where he was held. He would try to make the journey in two days. He asked his captors to give him a pass good for forty-eight hours, stating in writing that if he should be found off the direct route or outside of Brussels at the end of that period, he could be executed as a spy.

It was a dangerous proposal, but it gave him at least a hope of survival.

His revived confidence was severely shaken when a brusque officer came for him at midnight and took him in a car to a château which was evidently being used as a German headquarters. Men were hurrying through the halls, shouting that the English were making an attack on the German lines in the south. When the Germans saw the brown suit Davis wore, they cursed him, thinking he was a captive Englishman.

He sat in a gilded armchair with flashlights glaring upon him, guards looming over him. He thought he was finished. Sirens wailed in the darkness beyond the château.

The tall officer in the light blue uniform stormed into the room. The officer told Davis he would be set free under the terms he had proposed. Then the German smiled.

"You will start in three hours," the officer said.

Davis knew it was almost the equivalent of a sentence of death. If he went out into German-held territory in his brown suit at three in the morning, while the Germans were nervously awaiting the approach of British forces, he might be a target for the first trigger-happy sentry he encountered.

He protested, "You might as well take me out and shoot me now!"

The tall officer shrugged. "You will start in three hours."

Three hours later, the forty-eight-hour pass in his pocket, Davis started along the dark roads toward Brussels. He did not think he would live long enough to reach the city, but he had to try.

He had not gone far when a bright light blazed in his eyes and a guttural German voice ordered him to halt. He halted until the sentry had examined his pass. The soldier hesitated, then gestured roughly for him to move on.

The next time he was stopped, he struck a match to illuminate the red seal on his pass. The German had not flashed any light, and he ran the risk of death from a bullet when he struck the match. But Davis did not speak any German, and the red seal was the only means of communication he had.

He took the risk three times, and each time he was lucky enough to face a sentry who did not fire at him. But he was in a cold sweat. He knew such good fortune could not last all night.

When he came to a farmer's field, he crawled into a haystack and hid there until dawn.

Then, with one foot scraped raw and almost bare in a broken shoe, he dragged himself toward Brussels. German detachments stopped him often, read his pass, glared at him — and let him go on.

His foot gave him more and more pain. He had come to the point of deciding that he would never get to the capital city alive when he saw the automobile of a German general coming near him. He signaled, and the car stopped.

He explained what had happened to him. The general did not even trouble to look closely at his pass, but invited him to ride into Brussels. He was saved.

Richard Harding Davis had gone through the most dangerous adventure of his life. In the five wars he had covered in other years, he had never come so near to the brink of despair. His nerve had carried him through.

He had seen the German army in action. He had felt the savage power of imperialism on the march. And he raised his voice, in his remaining days, to arouse his fellow Americans to the menace of German might.

11 | Floyd Gibbons Risks His Life in a Submarine Zone

On a cold February day in 1917, an eighteen-thousand-ton British liner, the *Laconia,* steamed from New York Harbor, bound for France. She carried seventy-three passengers and a crew of more than two hundred men. One of her passengers, a stocky black-haired Irish reporter for the *Chicago Tribune,* had a feeling that the passengers and crew might never see a harbor again.

The big, fast-talking Irishman, Floyd Gibbons, had a hunch that the ship was doomed. A few weeks before she sailed, the Kaiser's government had announced that German submarines would send to the bottom of the ocean any ships traveling in the North Atlantic blockade zone. He believed the Germans meant what they said.

When the bulletins had come over the agency wires, announcing that the war in the Atlantic would take on new fury, the *Tribune* had decided to send Gibbons to England. He had already covered the fighting between American and Mexican forces on the Arizona border, Pancho Villa's Mexican revolution, and General Pershing's punitive expedition into Mexico. He had proved that he was bold, bright, and capable of taking care of himself in any emergency.

The *Tribune,* valuing Gibbons as a star reporter, wanted him to cross the Atlantic with Count von Bernstorff, the German ambassador, who was returning to Germany on the *Frederick VII.* But Gibbons wanted to find out what it was like to go into a war zone aboard a ship that might be torpedoed. He was willing to risk his life to get that story.

So he sailed on the *Laconia,* prepared to face whatever happened. He had been given some special equipment by the *Tribune,* to help him survive if he had to take to a lifeboat on the ocean — electric flashlights, a bottle for fresh water, a special life preserver, and a flask of brandy.

Gibbons knew that it would be a grim business to be in a lifeboat on the bitter Atlantic in midwinter, if he should be among the survivors of a submarine attack. But he had never flinched from hardship. He had led a rough-and-tumble life, and he'd found a way out of every corner.

With his quick grin, his fund of jokes, and his rapid-fire conversation, he made friends with many of the passengers during the first week of the voyage. The ship steamed peacefully ahead, the weather was generally fine, and no one seemed too much worried about the Kaiser's fleet of long gray sea-sharks.

Including Gibbons, there were six American citizens on the *Laconia* — two women from Chicago, a priest from Baltimore, a Mrs. Harris of Philadelphia, a man from New York, and the watchful reporter from the *Tribune*. There were a number of Englishmen — lawyers, diplomats, businessmen — and some of them had their wives and children with them.

On the eighth day of the trip — a Sunday — Gibbons asked the captain how far the ship had traveled, but got no information. His cabin steward, however, told him that the *Laconia* would be at Liverpool by Monday night. That indicated that the vessel was somewhere off the western coast of Ireland, and well within the submarine blockade zone.

Most of the passengers appeared to be very confident that the Germans would not dare to sink a passenger liner without warning — especially a ship carrying Americans. After the sinking of the *Lusitania* in 1915, the demands for war against Germany had risen so high in the United States that the Kaiser's government had called off its unrestricted submarine warfare. Relations between America and Germany were almost at the breaking point, and the torpedoing of another liner might bring America's power into the European conflict.

Nearly everyone seemed to think that the German commanders would certainly not enrage the civilized world by sinking a liner at this stage of the war. When there had been lifeboat drills — and there had been three of them in the eight days at sea — there had been a good deal of light talk about where the U-boats might be, but no one seemed to be really frightened.

That Sunday night, Gibbons was in the smoking room of the ship, standing near an open fireplace. At the card tables, some people were absorbed in bridge. In the lounge, the love song called "Poor Butterfly" came from a phonograph, and some couples were swinging around the dance floor.

Gibbons was with the man from New York, Arthur Kirby, and two Englishmen — a London lawyer, Henry Chetham, and Lucien J. Jerome of the British diplomatic service. He asked them to estimate what they considered "our chances of being torpedoed."

Mr. Chetham figured the odds at four thousand to one. Mr. Jerome thought the chances were two hundred and fifty to one that the vessel would not encounter a submarine.

While they were talking in that bright room, the dark waters of the Atlantic were being parted by a steel missile rushing toward the *Laconia*. Out of the cold dark sea, on that bitter February night, came an exploding instrument of destruction.

No signal of warning was given. Sliding under the sea,

the submarine had discovered the ship — and the ship was its prey, under the orders issued by the Kaiser's imperial government. The commander was a man who obeyed orders, whatever the world might think.

A few hours later, the world knew what had happened. Floyd Gibbons was one of the survivors rescued from the sea by a British minesweeper. The story he cabled to America aroused the indignation and wrath of millions.

He described what occurred when the signal came to abandon the ship — the five sharp blasts of the whistle:

We rushed down the corridor leading from the smoke room at the stern to the lounge, which was amidships. We were running, but there was no panic. The occupants of the lounge were just leaving by the forward doors as we entered.

It was dark on the landing leading down to the promenade deck, where the first-class staterooms were located. My pocket flashlight, built like a fountain pen, came in handy on the landing.

We reached the promenade deck. I rushed into my stateroom, B 19, grabbed my overcoat and the water bottle and special life preserver with which the *Tribune* had equipped me before sailing. Then I made my way to the upper deck on that same dark landing.

I saw the chief steward opening an electric switch box in the wall and turning on the switch. Instantly the boat decks were illuminated. That illumination saved lives.

The torpedo had hit us well astern on the starboard

side and had missed the engines and the dynamos. I had not noticed the deck lights before. Throughout the voyage our decks had remained dark at night and all cabin portholes were clamped down and all windows covered with opaque paint.

The illumination of the upper deck, on which I stood, made the darkness of the water, sixty feet below, appear all the blacker when I peered over the edge at my station boat, No. 10.

Already the boat was loading up and men and boys were busy with the ropes. I started to help near a davit that seemed to be giving trouble, but was stoutly ordered to get out of the way and get into the boat.

We were on the port side, practically opposite the engine well. Up and down the deck passengers and crews were donning life belts, throwing on overcoats, and taking positions in the boats. There were a number of women, but only one appeared to be hysterical — little Miss Titsie Siklosl, a French-Polish actress, who was being cared for by her manager. . . .

Steam began to hiss somewhere from the giant gray funnels that towered above. Suddenly there was a roaring swish as a rocket soared upward from the captain's bridge, leaving a comet's tail of fire. I watched it as it described a graceful arc in the black void overhead, and then, with an audible pop, it burst in a flare of brilliant colors.

There was a tilt to the deck. It was listing to starboard at just the angle that would make it necessary to reach for support to enable one to stand upright. In the meantime electric floodlights — large white enameled funnels containing clusters of bulbs — had been suspended from the promenade deck and illuminated the dark water that rose and fell on the slanting side of the ship.

"Lower away!" Someone gave the order, and we started down with a jerk towards the seemingly hungry rising and falling swells.

Then we stopped with another jerk and remained suspended in mid-air while the men at the bow and the stern swore and tussled with the lowering ropes. The stern of the lifeboat was down, the bow up, leaving us at an angle of about forty-five degrees. We clung to the seats to save ourselves from falling out.

"Who's got a knife, a knife, a knife!" shouted a sweating seaman in the bow. . . .

A hatchet was thrust into my hand and I forwarded it to the bow. There was a flash of sparks as it crashed down on the holding pulley. One strand of the rope parted and down plunged the bow, too quick for the stern man. We came to a jerky stop with the stern in the air and the bow down, but the stern managed to lower away until the dangerous angle was eliminated.

The list of the ship's side became greater, but instead of our boat sliding down it like a toboggan, the taffrail caught and was held. As the lowering continued, the other side dropped down and we found ourselves clinging on at a new angle and looking straight down on the water.

Many feet and hands pushed the boat from the side of the ship, and we sagged down again, this time smacking squarely on the pillowy top of a rising swell. It felt more solid than mid-air, at least. But we were far from being off. The pulleys stuck twice in their fastenings, bow and stern, and the one ax passed forward and back, and with it my flashlight, as the entangling ropes that held us to the sinking *Laconia* were cut away.

The boat finally got into the water. Then the crew members saw that the ship was turning over. One man went into a panic, screaming that when the water hit the *Laconia*'s hot boilers she would blow up — and the tons of shrapnel in the hold would be scattered over the sea around her.

Trying to keep everybody in the boat from surrendering to fear, Gibbons crawled to the stern, where he saw an old sea captain he had talked with often on the voyage from New York. He begged the captain to take command.

The captain said the rudder of the boat was gone, but he could steer with an oar. The old man agreed to take charge, but declared his voice was not strong enough to give orders. He said Gibbons would have to do the shouting.

There was only one way to get the attention of the crew. That was by an overpowering blast of profanity. I did my best and was rewarded by silence while I made the announcement that in the absence of the ship's officer assigned to the boat, Captain Dear would take charge.

We rested on our oars, with all eyes on the still lighted

Laconia. The torpedo had struck at 10:30 P.M., according to our ship's time. It was thirty minutes afterward that another dull thud, which was accompanied by a noticeable drop in the hulk, told its story of the second torpedo that the submarine had dispatched through the engine room and the boat's vitals from a distance of two hundred yards.

We watched silently during the next minute, as the tiers of lights dimmed slowly from white to yellow, then to red, and nothing was left but the murky mourning of the night, which hung over all like a pall. . . .

The ship sank rapidly at the stern until at last its nose stood straight up in the air. Then it slid silently down and out of sight like a piece of disappearing scenery in a panorama spectacle.

Boat No. 3 stood closest to the ship and rocked about in a perilous sea of clashing spars and wreckage. As the boat's crew steadied its head into the wind, a black hulk, glistening wet and standing about eight feet above the surface of the water, approached slowly and came to a stop opposite the boat and not six feet from the side of it.

"What ship was dot?" The correct words in throaty English with the German accent came from the dark hulk, according to Chief Steward Ballyn's statement to me later.

"The *Laconia*," Ballyn answered.

"Vot?"

"The *Laconia*, Cunard Line," responded the steward.

"Vot does she weigh?" was the next question from the submarine.

"Eighteen thousand tons."

"Any passengers?"

"Seventy-three," replied Ballyn. "Men, women and children, some of them in this boat. She had over two hundred in the crew."

"Did she carry cargo?"

"Yes."

"Vell, you'll be all right. The patrol will pick you up soon." And without further sound, save for the almost silent fixing of the conning-tower lid, the submarine moved off.

The patrol did not come soon. The lifeboat in which Gibbons rode, shouting the orders whispered to him by old Captain Dear, tossed and turned for six hours in the freezing night on the Atlantic before the bright beam of a searchlight came over the water.

With the other survivors, Gibbons was taken aboard the H.M.S. *Laburnum,* a mine sweeper, and brought to Queenstown. He hurried to a typewriter and then to a cable office.

On February 26, 1917, the report of Floyd Gibbons on the sinking of the *Laconia* hit the front pages. It appeared on the very day that President Woodrow Wilson told the Congress of the United States that Germany had not yet done an "overt act" that would require stern action by American forces.

The headlines on Gibbons's vivid description of a submarine attack on an unarmed vessel made it very clear to many Americans that the President's policy was not realistic. Whatever Woodrow Wilson might try to do to keep America out of the European war could not placate the militarists in Germany.

To the extremists in the German High Command, it seemed logical and necessary to sink any ships found in the zone around Great Britain and France which had been declared a combat area. They did not see how they could make any distinction between neutral ships and other vessels, if the ships were operating in a war zone.

War was war, in the opinion of the Kaiser's strategists. When nations were fighting, all the people of those nations were involved — men, women, and children. Countries trading with nations at war had to do so at their own risk. Any ship entering a battle area ran the risk of being sunk.

This idea of total war was difficult for the American President to accept. He could not believe, for a long time, that the German war lords really meant what they said.

Floyd Gibbons's story of the sinking of the *Laconia* brought the truth about the ruthless war in the Atlantic home to Americans who had not realized the actual nature of the submarine attacks.

With relentless efficiency, the Kaiser's U-boats went on smashing unarmed ships without warnings. And a few weeks after the torpedoing of the *Laconia,* after the destruction of three unarmed American vessels, the United States entered the war.

Gibbons, who had gambled his life in the submarine zone to get one of the most significant stories of the war, went to France and into battle with American troops.

Without a gun, he was with the U. S. Marines when they charged the German lines in Belleau Wood — and a German machine-gun bullet deprived him of one eye.

He was not daunted by that wound, any more than he had been daunted by the torpedo which struck the *Laconia* that night in the North Atlantic. He proved himself to be one of the great reporters of the First World War.

Under Fire in Italy, Hemingway Finds He Is Mortal

His officer's cap on the back of his head, the young Red Cross lieutenant rode a bicycle along a narrow road in Italy on a day in July, 1918. Husky and heavily tanned, he was a big and buoyant American, full of laughter, with a round open face creased from much smiling. He carried with him packages of chocolate, cigars, cigarettes, and postcards for the Italian troops in the trenches along the Piave River.

As he came closer to the front, the rumbling of artillery and the wham-wham of trench mortars told him that he was entering the area of danger. His mouth grew dry and his muscles tensed with excitement, but he pedaled more rapidly, eager to reach the battle line. He had traveled five thousand miles, from the middle of America to the northern provinces of Italy, to take part in this war.

The air smelled sweet; the world was bright around him. He was two weeks short of his nineteenth birthday; he was strong and healthy; and he did not believe that any enemy shells could ever touch him. He had been in the trenches when shells had burst, wounding and killing Italian soldiers around him, and he had not suffered a wound.

The Italians thought his life was protected by a charm, a thing of magic. He had seen the wounded crying in the mud; he had loaded men into ambulances; he had seen the dead lying with blank faces. But the shells had never harmed him. He did not believe he would ever be the way the wounded were — silent and crumpled, weeping and praying, or yelling at the sky.

He was young and surging with life. He could never be struck down. He was there to help the men who fell.

He was Ernest Hemingway, of Oak Park, Illinois — a wanderer, an amateur boxer, an ex-reporter for the *Kansas City Star*. He had tried a dozen times to get into the American armed forces, but had been turned down because of defective vision. One of his eyes had been injured in a boxing match.

He wasn't fit to fight, but he had reached the front. In April, he had found an item on the *Star's* telegraph desk, declaring that the Red Cross was seeking ambulance drivers for the Italian army. With Ted Brumback, another *Star* reporter who had suffered an eye injury, he had volunteered for service in Italy.

With Brumback, he had crossed the Atlantic late in

May on an old French Line ship which made the voyage without any destroyer escorts and managed to avoid the German submarines. He had hoped to see action in the Atlantic, and had been disappointed when there was no submarine attack.

In Paris he had found his first excitement, his first taste of the war. With Brumback, he reached the French capital during the bombardment of the city by the German long-range cannon called Big Bertha. They hired a taxi to chase the falling shells, hurrying through Paris for more than an hour.

At last they saw a direct hit. They saw a shell smash into the façade of the Madeleine, knocking off some of the stone of that great building. Brumback pictured the scene later: "No one was hurt. We heard the projectile rush overhead. It sounded as if it were going to land right in the taxi with us."

The shell did not land in the taxi. It passed over, as many other shells passed over Hemingway. He did not believe there was any shell with his number on it.

He had not come to Europe to chase around Paris in a taxicab. He wanted to get to the front. He was chafing and impatient after a few days in France, and was glad when the Red Cross sent him to Italy. That was the place where he wanted to be. That was the place where he would find the fighting he sought.

In Milan, Hemingway and Brumback went on emergency duty to carry out the wounded and the dead from a devastated munitions factory which had exploded. That was bitter work and terrible work, but it was not part of war as he thought of war. It was a disaster, but it was not a battle.

Then he was sent with a group of twenty-one other ambulance drivers to Schio, ninety miles east of Milan. The town was being shelled when Hemingway and Brumback arrived, but the bombardment was soon finished and a period of quiet followed.

The unit to which Hemingway belonged then had quarters in an abandoned mill near a stream which was good for swimming. Beyond the mill was a big meadow which the American ambulance men converted into a baseball field.

When Hemingway and the other drivers were not going to pick up wounded in the mountains above Schio, they went swimming or played baseball.

There was not enough action for Hemingway in the Schio sector. The mountains were beautiful and the swimming was fine and the baseball was fine, but he had not crossed the Atlantic to look at mountains or to go swimming or to play baseball day after day. He believed that this war was a crusade for democracy, and he had come to take an active part in it.

Later he might write scornfully of words like "honor" and "glory," but now he was a crusader.

When he had learned that volunteers were needed to run the Red Cross canteens on the Piave front, Hemingway offered to go at once. The canteens were close to the battle line, and he felt that he could get to the front every day, although the Red Cross officers in the canteens were not supposed to go to the trenches.

The combat troops in the line were allowed to visit the canteens several times a week for a little rest, a chance to write letters, to drink hot coffee or chocolate, to sit around smoking and relaxing. The canteens were comfortable, although not always quiet and peaceful, being often within the range of artillery fire from the Austrian guns.

Hemingway formed friendships with the Italian officers in the units near his canteen, and got invitations to visit the men in the trenches. That was what he had been seeking. The blazing heart of the war was there, where the weary troops stood in the mud.

Now he rode his bicycle directly to the front line. His friends saw him coming. Their faces brightened. They waved and laughed, knowing that he always brought cigars or cigarettes, chocolate or postcards, things they needed to relieve the fearful monotony of the trenches.

Hemingway was a genial American, and they shouted greetings to him. They called him the *giovane Americano,*

They knew that he did not have to come to the front. They knew that he came to help them, to share their troubles, to stand in the line with them.

On this day, July 8, Hemingway stayed late in the trenches near the small village of Fossalta. When darkness fell, he was still there, talking with his friends.

He was invited to go out to a listening post on the bank of the river. There he could hear the Austrians talking. He would be close to the enemy. He would know how it felt to hear the voices of men whose duty it was then to try to kill men who spoke another language.

The night was black, lighted only once in a while by the fire glow of exploding shells. In the heavy darkness Hemingway went to the listening post.

He crouched down with the three Italians who were stationed there. They were pleased to have him there, and eager to get the chocolate he brought.

At midnight an Austrian trench-mortar shell dropped upon the listening post. It was the deadly kind of shell known as a *Minenwerfer,* or "ash can."

When that shell burst in that black night, Hemingway's charmed life was over. He was hurled into the deep darkness of unconsciousness. Two of the Italians with him were killed. The third was severely wounded; this man's screams were the first sounds Hemingway heard when he became conscious again.

What he did then, he did without thinking, without knowing that he did it. His body was riddled with pieces of steel — doctors later took 237 fragments of shell from his right leg alone — and he had lost forever the feeling that he could not be killed or wounded. He knew he was mortal.

He did not know how he could move. But he moved. He lifted the wounded Italian upon his back. He began to carry the man across the torn ground toward the Italian trenches.

His body was so damaged in so many places that it did not want to move. It did not have the strength to walk. But he drove it. He walked, and he carried another man upon his back.

As he approached the trenches, he was suddenly bathed in light. And the light was more terrible than the groaning darkness which had surrounded him. He was trapped in the beam of an Austrian searchlight. With the wounded man he carried, he was a big target.

A heavy-caliber Austrian machine gun began to cough and clatter behind him. Bullets began to smash into the earth near his feet. A bullet hit one of his feet and another bullet thudded into his knee.

In the glare of the light, with blood pouring from him in a hot stream, he kept walking and walking. He bent beneath the burden of the wounded man, but he did not let go.

The light blazed around him and the machine gun hammered the ground he walked on.

He walked as far and as fast as he could. It was not very far and not very fast. But it was enough.

He made it into a first-aid dugout and collapsed. The Italian soldier he had carried with him was no longer breathing. The doctors began to dress Hemingway's wounds, without much hope for him.

After he came back to consciousness again, he was carried nearly two miles on a stretcher by Italian medical corpsmen. The road on which the stretcher-bearers moved away from the front was being shelled by Austrian artillery. Sometimes, when the shells exploded very near to them, the bearers dropped the stretcher and fell flat on their faces.

When the stretcher hit the earth, Hemingway knew what agony was. His wounds were opened, and he was raked by the hard claws of pain.

Finally he was taken into a stable. He lay there for two hours, on the edge of death. He seemed to be beyond the place where doctors could give him any aid.

But he was not yet nineteen years old, and he had reserves of endurance, the reserves of his youth and his health. Something in him resolved that he would not die. He had many things to do, and he was going to do them.

His charmed life was over, but he had a new life to live. His belief in the immortality of his body was gone, but there might be other ways of being more than mortal.

He was taken in an Italian ambulance to another dressing station and then to a field hospital, where he lay five days before he could be transferred to a base hospital in Milan. The doctors were busy, day after day, pulling pieces of steel from his flesh.

He had a dozen operations, and came through them all, able to joke about them. In a letter he wrote after six weeks in the hospital, he said, "I wouldn't really be comfortable now unless I had some pain."

Years later, in an introduction to a book called *Men at War,* Hemingway wrote:

> When you go to war as a boy you have a great illusion of immortality. Other people get killed; not you. . . . Then when you are badly wounded the first time you lose that illusion and you know it can happen to you. After being severely wounded . . . I had a bad time until I figured it out that nothing could happen to me that had not happened to all men before me. Whatever I had to do men had always done.

What he had to do, he decided, was to live by a code of absolute honesty, to face the violence and evil in the world without flinching, and to tell the truth about things as he saw them. He meant to be a writer who would be a great reporter and yet more than a reporter — looking deeper into things that reporters passed quickly over.

When he returned to the United States in January, 1919, he was interviewed by the *New York Sun* and depicted as a veteran "with probably more scars than any other man, in or out of uniform, who defied the shrapnel of the Central Powers." The interview revealed that Hemingway was planning a career as a writer.

He said he was "qualified to take a job on any New York newspaper that wants a man that is not afraid of work and wounds." He still limped from the wounds he had suffered at Fossalta, and he walked with the help of a cane, but he was sure that he could compete with any of the reporters New York had to offer.

He didn't get a job on a New York paper. He went home to Oak Park and made a speech at a high school assembly, describing his war wounds and holding up part of the shrapnel-torn uniform he had worn that night in Italy. The students in the audience never forgot his description of the war on the Italian front.

Later he went up to Michigan, to fish, to read, and to try to write. One of his friends, Carl Edgar, said afterward that Hemingway had come back from the war "figuratively as well as literally shot to pieces. He seemed to have a tremendous need to express the things he had felt and seen."

Perhaps his memories of the war were at first too painful for him to master. Perhaps his skill as a writer had not reached the stage of proficiency which would enable him to say what he wanted to say. He wrote story after story, and could not sell anything.

He was restless and unhappy. He found it hard to sleep at night. He had bad dreams, in which he repeated the whole experience of the explosion in the listening post, the wounds opening in his body, the merciless searchlight blazing upon him, the machine gun hammering at him, seeking to destroy him.

He wanted to get away from his home town. A friend of his father's, Ralph Connable, offered him an opportunity to live in Toronto. He leaped at the chance. He became a feature writer for the *Toronto Star,* whose editor was constantly looking for new young writers with talent.

In Toronto he did well from the beginning. In 1921 he went to Europe as a correspondent for the *Star,* basing his activities in Paris. And in Paris he found many people like himself, men and women whose lives had been damaged and crippled by the war.

He put some of them into his first successful novel, *The Sun Also Rises,* which came out in 1926 and made him famous. He had developed his own style — a spare, taut, bitter way of writing which was exactly the right style for the stories he wanted to tell.

In this book he freed himself from some of the pain of his wounds. He got rid of some of his nightmares. He painted the postwar world as it looked to a wounded young man — a young newspaperman in Paris, who had been through the same kind of agony Hemingway had suffered at Fossalta in 1918.

Under fire in Italy, he had lost the careless joy of his youth. But he still had the desire for immortality, and he wrote with a fierce energy, a tremendous determination to write so well that some of the things he created in words would last as long as the world.

"I died then," he said once, speaking of that night on the riverbank when the shell exploded in the listening post.

But he came back from the darkness into which he had been hurled. And out of that darkness he brought with him a volcanic fire of creation which flamed high in his books — in *The Sun Also Rises, A Farewell to Arms, For Whom the Bell Tolls, The Old Man and the Sea,* and all his works.

13 | Winchell Takes a Murderer into Captivity

On a hot night early in August, 1939, a telephone rang in the New York office of a sharp-eyed reporter whose breathless voice and hectic style were known to more Americans than any other newspaperman in the United States. With a restless sweep of one arm, Walter Winchell picked up the phone and snapped, "Winchell speaking."

In his columns and his radio broadcasts he ranged over every topic, from the pregnancies of movie stars to the President's latest appointments. He could never tell what would come over a telephone wire. He got calls from the White House, the FBI, Congressmen, judges, lawyers, race-track touts, press agents, people of all kinds. The calls came at all hours of the day and night, carrying bits of gossip, tips on coming events, warnings of danger, threats of blackmail.

He was interested in everything, and everybody knew it. When he answered the phone, he gave his name and waited.

On this hot night in August — the night of Saturday, August 5, 1939 — the caller said, "Don't ask me who I am. I have something important to tell you. Lepke wants to come in."

Winchell knew then that he had a big one on the end of his line. If he could engineer the surrender of Louis "Lepke" Buchalter, the shy, small man who was the top racketeer in New York, he would have the scoop of the year and one of the greatest achievements of his career. Lepke was supposed to be the head of Murder, Inc., the most ruthless ring of killers in American history.

The FBI was looking for Lepke. So was District Attorney Thomas E. Dewey. So were the police in the city and the state.

At Dewey's request, the Board of Estimate of New York City had posted a reward of twenty-five thousand dollars for Lepke's capture "dead or alive." J. Edgar Hoover, director of the FBI, had offered a similar reward but had not specified whether Lepke had to be brought in dead or alive.

"Lepke wants to come in," said the voice on the phone. "But he's heard so many stories about what will happen to him, he can't trust anybody, he says. If he could find someone he can trust, he will give himself up to that person. The talk around town is that Lepke would be shot while supposedly escaping."

Winchell knew that Lepke had tried to make a deal with the authorities. Lepke seemed to feel that it was better to be taken by federal agents and face an indictment for narcotics smuggling than to be captured by Dewey's men on a murder charge. But Lepke remembered that John Dillinger, another gangster, had been killed by FBI men after being trapped at a movie theater.

"Does he trust me?" Winchell asked.

The voice spoke anxiously: "Do you really mean that?"

"Sure," Winchell said. "I'll tell John Edgar Hoover about it and I'm sure he will see to it that Lepke receives his constitutional rights and nobody will cross him."

Winchell was certain that Lepke knew about his friendship with the FBI director.

"O.K.," said the voice. "Put it on the air tomorrow night if you can get that promise."

The telephone clicked. The connection was broken.

Winchell wrote a paragraph for his Sunday-night radio broadcast. He addressed it to Lepke, and said he would try to get Lepke a safe delivery into the hands of the federal agents.

The next afternoon, Sunday, Winchell called J. Edgar Hoover and read him the paragraph he had written for the broadcast. Hoover said, "You are authorized to state that the FBI will guarantee it."

When Winchell went on the air that night, Hoover

and his chief assistant, Clyde Tolson, were in the radio studio. They stayed there until Winchell made his repeat broadcast to the Pacific Coast an hour later, hoping that another phone call would come from Lepke's associates.

For two nights after the broadcasts, Winchell received calls.

"You're doing very well," the voices said. "You'll hear more later. If he agrees to come in, he will do it through you. But he may change his mind. Good-by."

Then silence fell. Weeks went by, with no word from Lepke. Apparently the gangster had changed his mind, perhaps from fear of a betrayal.

After Winchell had almost abandoned hope of capturing Lepke, a stranger approached him one night at Fifty-third Street and Fifth Avenue, near the Stork Club.

"Where can you be reached on a pay-station phone in an hour?" the stranger muttered.

Winchell went to the nearest telephone booth. The stranger took the number and said, "This is about Lepke. This time it's important. Please be here in an hour."

The stranger hurried away, jumped in a cab, and departed toward the north. Winchell called Hoover.

The FBI director was angry. He snapped, "This is a lot of bunk, Walter. You are being made a fool of and so are we. If you contact those people again, tell them the time limit is up! I will instruct my agents to shoot Lepke on sight."

But an hour later, the telephone jingled. Winchell seized the receiver and spoke before the man on the other end of the wire had a chance to say a word.

"I just spoke to Hoover," Winchell said urgently. "He's fed up. If Lepke doesn't surrender by four P.M. tomorrow, Hoover says no consideration of any kind will ever be given him. For every day he stays away it may mean an extra two years added to his sentence."

The man on the other end broke in: "He's coming in, but you simply have to wait until he can arrange things. He's willing to come in, but it can't be tomorrow. Maybe the next night. Where can you be reached tomorrow night at six?"

Winchell gave him another telephone number. The delays and the shifting of plans were exasperating, but these things revealed clearly the desperation and terror which ruled Lepke's life. Surrounded by violence, Lepke was afraid that his end would come through violence.

The next night the call came through to Winchell promptly at six o'clock. But the voice of the caller did not sound like the voice of the man who had spoken the night before.

Winchell was told, "Drive up to Proctor's Theater in Yonkers."

Then Winchell hesitated. He might be thrusting himself into a circle of danger. He had no certainty that the men who had been calling him were actually Lepke's representatives. He might be driving into a deadly trap.

Yet the excitement of the chase had caught him. He could not let it drop. He got in his car and drove to Yonkers. Before he reached Proctor's Theater, a car filled with strangers pulled carefully along next to his. A voice said, "That's him."

It was a very hot night in August, and Winchell was sweating. He did not know what to expect. Presently a man got out of the crowded car, holding up a handkerchief. The handkerchief shielded the man's face. The man climbed into Winchell's car.

"Go to the drugstore on the corner of Nineteenth Street and Eighth Avenue," said the man with the handkerchief. "There are some phone booths there. Get in one and appear busy. About nine P.M. somebody will come up to you and tell you where to notify the G men to meet you."

At five minutes to nine, Winchell stopped his car in front of the drugstore. He went inside and ordered a Coca-Cola while waiting to go into one of the phone booths. He turned once to look through the open door.

He saw a stranger nodding to him, gesturing. He went outside again, joined the man, and walked to his car.

"Go back in there and tell Hoover to be at Twenty-eighth Street on Fifth Avenue between ten-ten and ten-twenty," the stranger said.

Winchell went in and called the FBI and gave the message to Hoover.

When he returned to his car, the stranger was at the wheel. The car moved slowly through the Manhattan streets, the stranger glancing from side to side. The car went up and down Eighth Avenue, Ninth and Tenth avenues, in and out of side streets, down to Fourteenth, back to Twenty-third Street, and east to Madison Square.

More than an hour had passed. Winchell felt that he had butterflies fluttering in his stomach. Suddenly the stranger stepped from the car, after putting on the brakes.

"Just wait here," the stranger said. "And good luck."

Winchell took the wheel while the man walked swiftly away.

Winchell sat in the car, his clothes dripping with perspiration. He was trembling with tension.

A small neatly dressed man with heavy spectacles came hurrying up to the car. It was Lepke. Lepke opened the door, slid in, and said, "Hello. Thanks very much."

Winchell released the brakes and stepped on the gas. "We'll be with Mr. Hoover in a minute or two," Winchell said. "He's waiting in his car at Twenty-eighth Street."

"Yes, I know," said Lepke. "I just passed him."

Winchell drove slowly north on Fourth Avenue and then went on Twenty-seventh Street to Fifth Avenue. There he had to stop for a red traffic light — and there were two police cars, also halted by the red light.

The presence of the two police cruisers was a coincidence, but Lepke found it hard to understand. Lepke ripped off the spectacles he was wearing and tossed them to the sidewalk. The glasses broke with a crash. Two pedestrians who were passing stared upward at the buildings overhead, apparently believing that a window had been broken.

But the policemen in the patrol cars paid no attention. The lights changed, the police cruisers moved on, and Winchell drove the president of Murder, Inc., to Twenty-eighth Street and Fifth Avenue. Hoover sat at that intersection, in a government limousine. The FBI chief carried no arms or handcuffs, but wore dark glasses to keep passers-by from recognizing him.

Winchell parked his car behind an automobile which was just behind Hoover's limousine. He took Lepke over to the big black government car.

Keeping his voice calm, Winchell introduced them. "Mr. Hoover," he said, "this is Lepke."

With the prize in sight, Hoover was very affable.

"How do you do?" said the director of the FBI to the gangster he had been hunting for more than two years.

"Glad to meet you," said Lepke. "Let's go."

Hoover gave a command to the chauffeur of the limousine. "To the Federal Building on Foley Square," he ordered.

Lepke seemed eager to talk, to sit back and relax after years of being in flight. He spoke rapidly and excitedly. He was glad it was all over, but he was worried about what would happen to him.

"You did the smart thing by coming in, Lepke," Hoover assured him.

"I'm beginning to wonder if I did," Lepke answered. "I would like to see my wife and kids, please?"

Hoover promised that he would have an opportunity to talk to his family and kept the promise later that night, after Lepke had been booked and fingerprinted at the Federal Building.

Hoover asked Winchell, "Walter, what can I do for you?"

"First of all, this reward isn't going to be paid to anybody," Winchell answered. "This is my gift to the government. I'll take a one-edition beat. I don't want to be greedy."

When the government car got to Fourteenth Street,

on its way to Foley Square, Winchell got out and hurried to a telephone to make sure that his paper, the *New York Daily Mirror,* had the news of Lepke's surrender one edition earlier than any other paper in New York.

It was a big story, and the editor realized it. But it came on the night of August 25, when Germany and Poland were moving toward war, and the world was on the edge of a tremendous conflict.

"A fine thing!" groaned the *Mirror* editor. "With a world war starting!"

The paper was packed with news that night. Winchell had his scoop, far ahead of any rivals, and International News Service carried his eyewitness story on the surrender of Lepke. It made headlines in cities across the nation. This account is based on his story.

Winchell, who had been trying to lose weight for some time without much success, discovered that he had dropped six pounds and an inch from his waistline during the two days and nights of tension immediately preceding Lepke's surrender.

The fast-moving, fast-talking columnist received acclaim from leading citizens and many newspapers for his part in bringing a dangerous gangster into captivity. Among others, the *Brooklyn Eagle* declared that Winchell had accomplished "an outstanding public service, for which the community should be grateful."

Winchell went on to more scoops and more fame as a reporter, as a broadcaster on radio and television, and as an international figure crusading against bigotry, crime, and totalitarians of all types. He fought Fascists and Communists with equal vigor. While he was a sensational gossip hunter, he was also a thoughtful commentator on many aspects of American life and he was quoted everywhere.

After many court battles, Lepke died in the electric chair in Sing Sing prison on March 5, 1944, a little less than five years after the August night when Winchell took him to the government limousine on Fifth Avenue where J. Edgar Hoover was waiting for him.

14 | Edward R. Murrow Sees a Great Change in Britain under the Bombs

NIGHT AFTER NIGHT, in the blazing summer and early fall of 1940, a deep, steady voice came over the Atlantic Ocean from England to America, telling of England's battle for survival under the waves of German bombers. This strong and steady voice, an American voice with a slight accent of North Carolina, belonged to Edward R. Murrow, head of the European staff of the Columbia Broadcasting System.

"This is London," said Murrow, while the bombs fell and flames crackled in the streets of the city. His voice had a tone of sorrow for the suffering of that ancient city, and a tone of confidence, too, a feeling of belief that London would be there, no matter what it had to endure. It could not be destroyed.

Murrow had been in London for some years, and he knew the people of that immense place. He had seen them go through the Munich crisis of 1938, making jokes about their gas masks and digging trenches in the parks, stoically facing whatever might come. He had seen them cheering Neville Chamberlain when that bumbling Prime Minister made a pact with Hitler and Mussolini for "peace in our time." He had seen them ready to fight when Hitler marched in Poland in 1939 and England plunged into the Second World War.

Now he saw the British people suffering and standing firm under the rain of bombs from the Nazi air force. After conquering France, Hitler had given Britain a breathing spell, giving the British a chance to sue for terms before he set out to obliterate them. Under Winston Churchill, the British had defied him to do his worst.

Churchill put it plainly: "This wicked man, this monstrous product of former wrongs and shame, has now resolved to break our famous island race by a process of indiscriminate slaughter and destruction." To Churchill and to millions of other Englishmen, it was unthinkable that Hitler could succeed. It was unthinkable to Edward Murrow, too.

The heavy raids began in the middle of August, when the barrage of Nazi bombs started to fall along England's Channel coast. The German bombers cast dark shadows over the white cliffs of Dover, and England's Home Guard prepared to fight on the beaches, on the cliffs, in the hills, until the last Englishman died or the invaders were driven off.

Air Marshal Goering's bomber pilots were cocksure of their eventual triumph over England. The Nazis remembered that they had set fire to Warsaw and wiped out the heart of Rotterdam. The fate of these two cities lay in store for London, Hitler and Goering believed. And when London was a burned city of wreckage, England would go under.

But the English were more fortunate than the Poles in Warsaw and the Dutch in Rotterdam. They had the English Channel as a barrier against the Nazi ground forces, and they had the Royal Air Force, equipped with magnificent Spitfires, to battle the Nazis in the sky.

The ordeal of London really started in the first week of September, when the infuriated Hitler was at last convinced that the English did not intend to give in. On September 7, 1940, nearly four hundred German bombers roared over the city in broad daylight. Marshal Goering boasted, "This is the historic hour when our air force for the first time delivered its stroke right into the enemy's heart."

Fires flamed, houses crumbled, gas mains burst, a pall of smoke rose from the streets. Men, women, and children felt the cruel lash of the bombs. Sirens wailed, ambulances rushed from one place of agony to another, and fire fighters faced the flames hour after hour.

It seemed impossible for any city to take so much punishment and continue to endure. It seemed impossible for the people of the city to do their daily jobs, to work and eat and sleep and carry on the business of life, with the crash of bombs all around them and planes spitting fire in the skies above them.

But the city endured. Trains brought commuters in from the suburbs. Buses rumbled along the bomb-pocked streets. The fires were brought under control. Bottles of milk arrived on doorsteps, and women took them in, just as if the war was a thousand miles away. Newspapers appeared and people bought them, hurrying to work and reading reports of the battle raging over London.

And Edward R. Murrow went on the air, saying in his deep, steady voice, "This is London. . . ." He spoke as though nothing could ever keep him from saying those words, which told the world that the capital of the British Empire was still alive. He did not speak them with any bravado, with any attempt to sound heroic. He simply voiced the quiet truth of the city's existence.

A tall, dark-haired man with a saturnine, handsome face, a quizzical smile, and a cigarette always between his lips, Murrow seemed utterly indifferent to danger. He took his chances with the millions in London. He came close to death several times when bombs exploded near him, but he went on with his job — just as the bus drivers and the barbers and the newsboys of London went on with theirs.

Members of Britain's aristocracy admired Murrow and sought his company. He was at home with dukes and duchesses, and the leaders of the nation — including Winston Churchill — valued his comments.

But he knew that Britain's fate depended upon the stamina of the people in the shops and streets, the men in the pubs, the housewives, the fire watchers on the roofs, the volunteer stretcher-bearers, the people who had a thousand difficult and painful things to do.

Much depended upon the handful of fliers who rose day after day and night after night to meet the swarms of Nazi bombers. The men in the R.A.F. reached the limits of exhaustion and then went beyond those limits, still fighting.

But the people of London were also in the front lines — and they did not have the satisfaction of being able to fight back. They couldn't reach up and smash the enemy planes. They had to dig frantically in cellars to rescue their friends who had been buried under wreckage. They had to stamp out endless fires. They had to stand firm and take whatever the enemy threw at them.

If their spirit was sound, Britain would survive. If they

faltered and failed at last, all the boldness and bravery of Churchill, all the sacrifices of the R.A.F. and the Navy, guarding the English Channel, would be of no avail.

Murrow saw them standing firm, but no one could be certain of how long they would stand. He went out to talk to the people while the German bombers roared overhead. And he found that a great change was going on — a change in the fundamental attitudes of a people long accustomed to certain ways of doing things.

By sensing and describing this change — which was as important in British history as the battle in the sky and the struggle to save London — Murrow proved his ability as a reporter who looked beneath the surface of events.

In a broadcast to America on September 15, 1940, he began to describe what was happening. He tried to tell his fellow Americans, so far away from the bombs and the fires, of the cry for equality rising from the British people.

Murrow said:

During the last week you have heard much of the bombing of Buckingham Palace and probably seen pictures of the damage. You have been told by certain editors and commentators who sit in New York that the bombing of the palace, which has one of the best air-raid shelters in England, caused a great surge of determination — a feeling of unity — to sweep this island.

The bombing was called a great psychological blunder. I do not find much support for that point of view amongst Londoners with whom I've talked. They don't like the idea of their King and Queen being bombed, but remember, this is not the last war — people's reactions are different. Minds have become hardened and callused. It didn't require a bombing of Buckingham Palace to convince these people that they are all in this thing together.

There is nothing exclusive about being bombed these days. When there are houses down in your street, when friends and relatives have been killed, when you've seen that red glow in the sky night after night, when you're tired and sleepy — there just isn't enough energy left to be outraged about the bombing of a palace.

The King and Queen have earned the respect and admiration of the nation, but so have tens of thousands of humble folk who are much less well protected. If the palace had been the only place bombed, the reaction might have been different. Maybe some of those German bomb aimers are working for Goebbels instead of Goering, but if the purpose of the bombings was to strike terror to the hearts of the Britishers, then the bombs have been wasted.

That fire bomb on the House of Lords passed almost unnoticed. I heard a parcel of people laughing about it when one man said, "That particular bomb wouldn't seriously have damaged the nation's war effort."

I'm talking about those things not because the bombing of the palace appears to have affected America more than Britain, but in order that you may understand this war has no relation with the last one, so far as symbols and civilians are concerned.

You must understand that a world is dying, that old values, the old prejudices, and the old bases of power and prestige are going. In an army, if the morale is to be good, there must be equality in the ranks. The private with money must not be allowed to buy himself a shelter of steel and concrete in the front-line trench. One company can't be equipped with pitchforks and another with machine guns.

London's civilian army doesn't have that essential quality — I mean equality of shelter. One borough before the war defied the authorities and built deep shelters. Now people arrive at those shelters from all over town and the people who paid for them are in danger of being crowded out. Some of those outsiders arrive in taxis, others by foot. Since it's a public shelter they can't be barred by the people whose money went into the digging. This is just one of the problems in equality that London is now facing.

Murrow went on to depict the other troubles facing the people of the city.

There are the homeless from the bombed and fire-blackened East End area. They must be cared for, they must be moved, they must be fed, and they must be sheltered.

Murrow listened to what the people of London were saying while they fought fires, rescued the injured, and worked grimly to keep their city alive under the Nazi rain of bombs.

He reported to America:

The people have been told that this is a people's war, that they are in the front lines, and they are. If morale is to be maintained at its present high level, there must be no distinction between the troops living in the various sections of London.

When Murrow walked the bomb-torn streets, he saw that some of the old buildings, the historic places of London, had been destroyed. The roar of antiaircraft guns, the rattle of machine guns on planes fighting overhead mingled with the crashing thunder of great buildings going down — buildings with centuries of tradition behind them.

While he wrote his broadcasts, the windows trembled in the room where he sat, and he kept candles and matches near his typewriter for use when the electric lights went out. When he went to dinner in a restaurant with friends, the headwaiter took them to a table away from windows. Splinters of flying glass from windows broken by blasts of explosions were as deadly as bullets or bombs.

Murrow saw London being lacerated and mutilated. He saw the face of the city changing — and the people changing with it. And he learned that the strength of Britain was not so much in its traditions, its ancient towers, its mighty castles as in the quiet, stubborn people who clenched their hands and set their teeth and would not quit.

In a broadcast on October 1, 1940, he summed up what was occurring in a phrase that later became famous: "There is occurring in this country a revolution by consent."

He declared:

Millions of people ask only, "What can we do to help? Why must there be eight hundred thousand unemployed when we need these shelters? Why can't the unemployed miners dig? Why are new buildings being constructed when the need is that the wreckage of bombed buildings be removed from the streets? What are the war aims of this country? What shall we do with victory when it's won? What sort of Europe will be built when and if this stress has passed?"

These questions are being asked by thoughtful people in this country. Mark it down that in the three weeks of the air *Blitz* against this country more books and pamphlets have been published on these subjects than in any similar period of the war. Remember also that I am permitted to record this plan of political and social salvation at a time when this country fights for its life.

Mark it down that these people are both brave and patient, that all are equal under the bomb, that this is a war of speed and organization, and that the political system which best provides for the defense and decency of the little man will win. . . .

Murrow's prophecy of eventual victory for the side with the best provisions for the ordinary people of the world proved to be accurate. The early triumphs of the Axis powers were obliterated by the final triumphs of the Allied nations.

Three years after Goering's air force launched its savage attacks on London, the British were giving Berlin the kind of treatment London had received — with heavier bombs and more devastation. The patient Englishmen who had taken so much punishment were determined to teach the Germans that bombing of cities brought a terrible vengeance.

In one of the British bombers, on a night early in December, 1943, rode Edward R. Murrow — determined to see what a bombing looked like to the men in the sky.

He went in a black four-motored Lancaster bomber named *D for Dog*. The plane was one of hundreds converging on Berlin. Like others, it was caught by German searchlights, fired on by Berlin's antiaircraft batteries, and attacked by fighter planes.

On that raid, forty-one British bombers were shot down. Out of the group of reporters who went with the raiders, just two men returned. One of the two was Murrow.

In a broadcast carried throughout the United States on December 3, 1943, Murrow described his flight.

In a little more than half an hour, Berlin had received about three times the weight of bombs that had ever fallen on London in the course of a long winter night.

He saw the capital of Germany blazing with thousands of fires.

The small incendiaries were going down like a fistful of white rice thrown on a piece of black velvet. As Jock [the wing commander in charge of the bomber] hauled the *Dog* up again, I was thrown to the other side of the cockpit, and there below were more incendiaries, glowing white and then turning red. The cookies — the four-thousand-pound high explosives — were bursting below like great sunflowers gone mad. And then, as we started down again, still held in the lights, I remembered that the *Dog* still had one of those cookies and a whole basket of incendiaries in his belly and the lights still held us. And I was very frightened.

While Jock was flinging her about in the air, he suddenly flung over the intercom, "Two aircraft on the port beam." I looked astern, and saw Wally, the mid-upper, whip his turret around to port and then look up to see a single-engined fighter slide just above us. The other aircraft was one of ours.

Finally we were out of the searchlight cone, flying level. I looked down on the white fires, the white fires had turned red. They were beginning to merge and spread, just like butter does on a hot plate. . . .

The bomber dropped its four-thousand-pound "cookie" filled with high explosives, and got rid of all its smaller incendiary bombs except one small container.

We saw more battles. Then another plane in flames. But no one could tell whether it was ours or theirs. We were still near the target. Dave, the navigator, said, "Hold her steady, skipper, I want to get an astral sight." And Jock held her steady. And the flak began coming up at us. It seemed to be very close. It was winking off both wings. But the *Dog* was steady. Finally Dave said, "O.K., skipper, thank you very much." And a great orange blob of flak smacked up straight in front of us. And Jock said, "I think they're shooting at us." I'd thought so for some time.

And he began to throw *D for Dog* up, around, and about again. And when we were clear of the barrage, I asked him how close the bursts were, and he said, "Not very close. When they're really near, you can smell them." That proved nothing, for I'd been holding my breath.

Jack sang out from the rear turret, said his oxygen was getting low, thought maybe the lead had frozen. Titch, the wireless operator, went scrambling back with a new mask and a bottle of oxygen. Dave, the navigator, said, "We're crossing the coast."

My mind went back to the time I had crossed the coast in 1938, in a plane that had taken off from Prague. Just ahead of me sat two refugees from Vienna — an old man and his wife. The copilot came back and told them that we were outside German territory. The old man reached out and grasped his wife's hand.

The work that was done last night was a massive blow of retribution for all those who have fled from the sound of shots and blows on a stricken continent.

Murrow saw the German people paying, in blood and agony, for the crimes of Hitler and the Nazis. The war had come full circle — from the Battle of Britain to the Battle of Germany.

Through his broadcasts, Edward R. Murrow brought the meaning of the war closer to the American people. Through his reporting, they felt the march of history.

15 | Ernie Pyle Learns That Americans Have the Strength of Spartans

Even in his heavy underwear, even with two sweaters and an overcoat and heavy gloves, even with two pairs of socks on his feet and thick boots over the socks, the thin man with the elfin face was cold all the time. There were shells exploding and bombs whistling down from the air, and machine guns made a bitter chatter in North Africa, in November of 1942, but the thing that bothered everybody all the time was the constant cold. And the thin man, whose name was Ernest Taylor Pyle, suffered more than most of the men in the foxholes because he had no fat to keep him warm: he was just a bag of skin and bones.

Ernie Pyle was a one hundred per cent American — he came from Indiana, from the heart of the farm country — and he knew how the men in the foxholes felt, because he got up there with them. Americans liked to be warm. Americans liked to be comfortable. Americans liked to be clean.

Nobody could keep really warm in the arid hills and plains of North Africa. Nobody could get really comfortable, if he happened to be a soldier and in the infantry. And nobody could keep clean when he had to sleep in his clothes day after day and had no place to take a bath.

And there was the problem of food. Americans came from a country with plenty of meat and plenty of potatoes and plenty of bread and gravy — plenty of everything. Americans knew there was plenty, and Americans liked to eat. Americans hated to be gaunt and skinny, and tortured by a gnawing sense of hunger.

But in North Africa the food often didn't get through. There were American artillerymen in the mountains who had to fight week after week on one cold meal a day. There were infantrymen who had to live week after week on hard chunks of stuff called K rations.

Ernie Pyle, the reporter from Indiana, knew just how they felt, because his stomach was rumbling, too. He always had a frost in his bones and he felt itchy because he wasn't able to get a bath for a month at a time. His knees creaked and his arms ached from sleeping on the ground.

He felt horribly homesick for all the wonderful things that were spread around for almost everybody in America — solid chairs and good lights and dining-room tables and tablecloths and clean plates. He missed all the stores with their bright crowded windows, so full of bedroom sets and radios and waffle irons and birch cabinets and beautiful rugs and hundreds of handy gadgets. Perhaps most of all he missed hot water.

Because he couldn't shave without hot water he grew a beard, as many of the soldiers did. But he felt strange with a beard — grimy and dirty and unkempt. Americans didn't grow beards, and didn't feel right with beards. Americans had smooth faces, closely shaven.

The soldier's world was a primitive world, where men lived as they had to live before the development of modern civilization — without houses, without comforts, with little food. To stand such a life, to endure it and survive, men had to develop the qualities of the Spartans of ancient Greece. The Spartans were sternly disciplined people who led a rigorous existence — a frugal, austere life.

The Nazis in North Africa did not believe the Americans could show the strength of Spartans. The battle-hardened combat troops of Hitler's *Panzer* divisions struck hard at the American lines in the first battles in Africa, confidently expecting the easygoing, comfort-loving troops from the U.S.A. to cave in under their blows.

The people in the United States, supremely sure that American boys were the best fighters in the world, were shocked and stricken when German divisions thrust the American forces backward in the battle of the Kasserine Pass early in 1943. Working in war factories, seeing the tanks and guns pouring from the assembly lines, the Americans at home felt that the war was a gigantic contest in production — and a country with the productive power of the U.S. was bound to win.

But it was more than that — it was a test of men. The young men from New York and Alabama, Maine and Texas, California and Florida, the teen-agers who had volunteered and the men who had been drafted from farms and cities in all the states, knew that it was a thing that tried the hearts and souls and inner strength of individual men who bore the brunt of it. And Ernie Pyle was with them, and learned that bloody lesson with them.

He was in Sbeitla, near the command post of the First Armored Division, when he heard of the German attack. He was digging a hole for his pup tent when the Nazi dive bombers came shrieking down upon the cactus patch where the command post stood. The hole was only a few inches deep, but Pyle leaped into it.

He shared and fully understood the confusion which overcame the American troops in the pass, the troops taken by surprise and confronted by hundreds of German tanks. He talked with dozens of officers and enlisted men who had retreated under the Nazi onslaught, and he nodded while they tried to tell him how it was.

"I'll bet I had that battleground scratched in the sand

for me fifty times," Pyle wrote in a column printed later by home-town newspapers all over America.

Men fell to the ground exhausted, and he saw Americans sleeping the furious sleep of men who had been driven until they were worn out. He, too, stretched upon the ground. Lying beside them, he shared their weariness and he never forgot it.

That afternoon the American tank forces gathered for a counterattack. Long lines of clanking machines came to the assembly points and then halted. Before the order to advance was given, the tanks reminded Ernie Pyle of "the cars lined up at Indianapolis just before the race starts — their weeks of training over, everything mechanically perfect, just a few minutes of immobility before the great struggle for which they had waited so long."

The machines were there, by the thousands, and brave men were there, with courage to face the enemy. But General Rommel had earned the name of the Desert Fox, and the Germans were veterans with much experience, skilled in maneuvers and trickery. Rommel's men won that day.

Advancing in their roaring, clanking lines, the American tanks were hit by a heavy barrage of German artillery shells. German tanks got in behind the American lines and began to smash up American trucks and jeeps. The

American counterattack was halted, and the Americans had to withdraw.

The next night, a full-fledged retreat was under way. The night was bitterly cold and black, and hail was falling from the dark sky of North Africa.

"It was hard to realize, when you were part of it, that this was a retreat — that American forces in large numbers were retreating in foreign battle — one of the few times in our history," Pyle wrote later. Participation in that retreat filled him with a terrible sadness.

He felt an overwhelming grief for all the young Americans lying in the barren gullies and desolate plains of North Africa. He felt sorry for the men at the front who wished they could be in safe berths behind the lines, and the men in safe berths who were eager to get to the front. He felt sorry for all the young men who had been brought up in optimism and comfort, young men who had been counting on a future filled with pleasant jobs and easy times — and then had to face the filth and the drudgery of war in this poverty-stricken country.

He was forty-two — thin, underweight, middle-aged, full of small ailments. He was not a fighting man. But he had felt an obligation to be with the fighting men, who needed somebody to talk to, somebody who might make the folks at home see what they were going through.

Cold and weary, he rode in his jeep all the way to Algiers. There he got a bed in the Aletti Hotel, had a long night's sleep in the soft warmth of a mattress, and woke in the morning in a room with solid walls around him. He then enjoyed the luxuries of a hot bath and a shave. He thought of what the combat men would have enjoyed — the simplest things of life away from the battle zone: a room with windows, the feeling of warm water, the sense of getting clean all over.

He learned that the Germans had been stopped after they had plunged twenty-one miles beyond the Kasserine Pass. A new commander was taking over the American forces in the Kasserine area — a big, swaggering, fearless man, General George S. Patton, Jr. Patton had the drive and the determination to whip an army into shape.

And the American army was far from defeated. It had lost a battle; it had been outmaneuvered by General Rommel and his wily veterans. But the men in that army had begun to harden under battle conditions — Americans showed that they had the strength of Spartans.

Ernie Pyle discovered an astonishing thing. In the Aletti Hotel in Algiers, where he could sleep as late as he wanted to, where he could get plenty of food cooked in a fairly appetizing style, where he had the comforts he had been yearning for, he did not feel as alive or alert as he had at the front. He got a bad cold, he coughed, he felt miserable.

There was something in the Spartan life that made a man feel close to the earth, close to reality. There was something in that life which gave a man a different feeling of strength and self-reliance — a sense of grim triumph, to be able to carry on day after day with only the bare necessities of human existence.

"The front does get into your blood, and you miss it and want to be back," he wrote to a friend, Lee Miller of the Scripps-Howard newspapers. "Life up there is very simple, very uncomplicated, devoid of all the jealousy and meanness that floats around a headquarters city, very healthful despite the cold, and time passes so damned fast it's just unbelievable. . . ."

He had to get back — back to the infantry, to the foot soldiers who were the loneliest men in the world up there walking toward the enemy.

He joined a battalion of the First Division in the hills near Mateur.

"I love the infantry because they are the underdogs," he wrote. "They are the mud-rain-frost-and-wind boys. They have no comforts, and they even learn to live without the necessities. And in the end they are the guys that wars can't be won without."

This time he spent a week living the life of a combat rifleman. He was under steady fire for three days and nights. He cowered in a foxhole at dawn, day after day,

while the Nazi dive bombers came over and raked the hills with death.

It was a wretched life. Several nights he slept on the ground without a blanket or a shelter half. No hot food could be brought up to the battle line, because of the intensity of the enemy bombardment. He ate cold rations out of torn tin cans, and drank cold coffee. And in the foxholes there were scorpions, snakes, lizards, reptiles in monstrous forms.

And yet that wretched life gave him a sense of being exalted — a high excitement he had never felt before. He wrote his columns in foxholes, with broken pieces of pencil on scraps of note paper, while machine gunners tried to get him.

Describing a line of troops emerging from a battle, he wrote:

The men are walking. They are fifty feet apart, for dispersal. Their walk is slow, for they are dead weary, as you can tell even when looking at them from behind. Every line and sag of their bodies speaks their inhuman exhaustion. On their shoulders and backs they carry heavy steel tripods, machine-gun barrels, leaden boxes of ammunition. Their feet seem to sink into the ground from the overload they are bearing.

They don't slouch. It is the terrible deliberation of each step that spells out their appalling tiredness. Their faces are black and unshaven. They are young men, but the grime and whiskers and exhaustion makes them look middle-aged. The line moves on, but it never ends. All afternoon men keep coming round the hill and vanishing eventually over the horizon. It is one long, tired line of antlike men. There is an agony in your heart and you almost feel ashamed to look at them.

They are just guys from Broadway and Main Street, but you wouldn't remember them. They are too far away now. They are too tired. Their world can never be known to you, but if you could see them just once, just for an instant, you would know that no matter how hard people work back home they are not keeping pace with these infantrymen in Tunisia.

But when the troops got a rest, they recovered more swiftly than Pyle had imagined they could. Their youth and their strength returned to them, after a little sleep, a little hot food, a few days away from the front.

And he found that they were proud of themselves. They had walked through the fires of war and they had proved that they were fighters equal in endurance with the battle-stained veterans of Rommel's desert rats. They knew the enemy respected them and feared them.

He wrote:

I sit around with them, and they get to telling stories, both funny and serious, about their battle. They are all disappointed when they learn that I am not permitted to name the outfit they're in, for they are all proud of it and would like the folks at home to know what they've done. "We always get it the toughest," they said.

The folks at home got over the shock of the American defeat in the Kasserine Pass. The new American army proved in the field that the comforts and luxuries of life in America had not destroyed the essential stamina of American youth.

American divisions roared across North Africa into Sicily and Italy with the Allied forces, and finally landed in Normandy to break down the iron walls of Hitler's Europe. And wherever the going was toughest, the GI's saw the thin little man with the tired, eager face — the middle-aged man from Indiana who was there to tell their story, to make sure that their heroism did not go without recognition.

Ernie Pyle was there when thousands of Americans got their reward for their Spartan endurance and their bravery in battle. He saw the liberation of Paris. In fact, he got into Paris ahead of the GI's; he shared the first hours of rejoicing with the French soldiers of General Le-Clerc's division, which was the first to enter the city. Pyle described it vividly:

I had thought that for me there could never again be any elation in war. But I had reckoned without the liberation of Paris — I had reckoned without remembering that I might be a part of this richly historic day. We are in

Paris — on the first day — one of the great days of all time. . . .

We drove through a flat, garden-like country under a magnificent bright sun and amidst greenery, with distant banks of smoke pillaring the horizon ahead and to our left. And then we came gradually into the suburbs, and soon into Paris itself. . . .

The streets were lined as by Fourth of July parade crowds at home, only this crowd was almost hysterical. The streets of Paris are very wide, and they were packed on each side. The women were all brightly dressed in white or red blouses and colorful peasant skirts, with flowers in their hair and big, flashy earrings. Everybody was throwing flowers, and even *serpentin.*

As our jeep eased through the crowds, thousands of people crowded up, leaving only a narrow corridor, and frantic men, women and children grabbed us and kissed us and shook our hands and beat on our shoulders and slapped our backs and shouted their joy as we passed. . . . We all got kissed until we were literally red in the face, and I must say we enjoyed it. Everybody, even beautiful girls, insisted on kissing you on both cheeks.

Somehow I got started kissing babies that were held up by their parents, and for a while I looked like a baby-kissing politician going down the street. The fact that I hadn't shaved for days, and was gray-bearded as well as bald-headed, made no difference.

It was a long road from the cold and barren plains and mountains of North Africa to the embraces and warm kisses of the people in Paris. Ernie Pyle traveled that road with the combat soldiers.

His arrival in Paris with the forces of liberation was the most joyous day Pyle experienced in his career as a war reporter. It was the day of triumph, the day of justification for all the sacrifices and suffering of the brave men who had fought so hard and endured so much along the way.

The collapse of Nazi Germany came a few months after the liberation of Paris, and Japan surrendered a little less than a year later. Ernie Pyle did not live to see the victory in the Pacific. He was killed by bullets from a Japanese machine gun on the small island of Ie-jima on April 18, 1945.

On the place where he was killed, American infantry-men erected a wooden marker, carrying these words:

AT THIS SPOT
THE 77TH INFANTRY DIVISION
LOST A BUDDY

ERNIE PYLE

18 APRIL 1945

This was later replaced by a monument bearing the same inscription.

| Maggie Higgins Takes Part
in the Liberation of Dachau's
Concentration Camp

Aᴸᴇʀᴛ in their watchtowers high above the prisoners'
compound, in the huge concentration camp in the
Bavarian city of Dachau, the SS guards stood fearfully
holding rifles and machine guns. With the weapons they
had in their huts on the towers, the guards held the thirty
thousand prisoners in subjection. But the sound of fighting came from the north, and the prisoners were beginning to walk boldly through the compound. The
guards in the towers were afraid: the feeling of liberation crackled in the air.

It was the spring of 1945 — one of the great times of
change and hope in the history of the world. The long
nightmare of the Second World War was ending in
Europe. Hitler's armies were falling to pieces. The prisoners at Dachau knew that their hour of release was near.

Their freedom came sooner than they had expected —
and it came through the daring of an American girl,
Maggie Higgins of the *New York Herald Tribune*. Tall

and blonde, energetic and relentless in pursuit of a story, Maggie was never satisfied to be simply at the front. She had to be ahead of the front, ahead of the American army, if she could get there — and she got there often.

On this bright April day, the girl came riding along the broad driveway leading to the entrance of the Dachau camp. She rode in a jeep with another correspondent who never hesitated to try anything once — Sergeant Peter Furst, an enlisted reporter serving the U. S. Army newspaper, *Stars and Stripes.*

The jeep was loaded with captured German weapons — rifles, pistols, and hand grenades. Ranging ahead of the American tanks, Higgins and Furst had already accepted the surrenders of dozens of husky German soldiers who were sick of the war. They had roared through villages that were full of white flags — and the Germans had cheered them on.

Sergeant Furst and Maggie Higgins had special reasons to spur them through Germany at a breakneck speed. Furst had been born in the Rhineland, and his family had been driven out of Germany when Fuehrer Hitler had begun attacks on the Jews. He was eager to see the collapse of Hitler's Germany, eager to take part in the liberation of the prisoners held in Hitler's death camps.

Maggie Higgins, who had been a reporter only a few years and a war correspondent only a short time, was eager to show the men correspondents in Europe what a girl could do. She came of Irish-French parentage, and she was not one to hold back from dangerous assignments.

She had already watched Sergeant Furst persuade the *Bürgermeister* of a German city to prepare the way for the surrender of the city to American forces. In a village near Augsburg, the third largest city in Bavaria, Higgins and Furst had found that telephone lines between the village and Augsburg were still functioning. When they got to the command post of Major General "Iron Mike" O'Daniel, commander of the U. S. Third Division, they found O'Daniel receptive to the idea of having Furst telephone the *Bürgermeister* to demand a surrender.

Furst made the call, the *Bürgermeister* said he would do everything he could to reduce the resistance, and Augsburg was captured without the loss of any American lives.

After that, when Sergeant Furst suggested that they roll ahead to see what was happening at Dachau, Maggie Higgins did not hesitate to go with him.

When they approached the gates of the enormous concentration camp at the outskirts of Dachau, they saw a German general wobbling beneath the weight of a large white flag. Next to the general stood a German in civilian clothes who declared that he was with the International Red Cross.

The girl from the *Herald Tribune* and the sergeant from *Stars and Stripes* assured the two Germans that some American officers would appear soon to accept their surrender. Their objective was to get to the prisoners' compound and open those gates.

They knew that the gates and the barbed-wire fence around the compound were electrified, and anyone who touched those barriers ran the risk of sudden electrocution. They needed someone to turn off the current.

In his fluent German, Sergeant Furst asked the general to order an SS officer to take Miss Higgins and himself to the compound. The general immediately obeyed.

The SS officer got into the jeep. Sergeant Furst and Maggie Higgins rode with him to the enclosure. As they came near to it, they saw the SS guards in the watchtowers.

They did not know whether the guards were ready to give up or whether the SS men had orders to fight to the end and would follow those orders. If the SS men fought, they did not have a chance of escaping with their lives. One burst from one of the machine guns above them would mean destruction for both of them.

When the jeep halted near the barbed wire, Maggie

Higgins jumped out. She wore a fur-lined hat with fur ear flaps, a fur-lined German army jacket she had found in a warehouse in Weimar, a pair of fatigue-duty army pants, and an army shirt. With her slim figure, she had the appearance of an American soldier — although she wore a German jacket.

The girl started around a corner of one of the buildings. Then she heard Sergeant Furst shouting, telling her to get back into the jeep. She saw that he was pointing upward toward something ahead of her.

She followed the direction in which Furst pointed. She saw a watchtower crowded with German soldiers. They had rifles and machine guns, and the weapons were aimed at her.

Something about her must have puzzled them. She had on some German clothes, and yet she was obviously not a German soldier. She walked with a careless, quick stride.

She did not do what Furst begged her to do. She did not turn or run. She tilted her head and spoke in her high-pitched voice to the SS guards in the tower.

In slow, careful German, she told them that Americans had arrived. She asked them to come over to where she was.

And the SS men came down from the tower meekly and brought their weapons to her. Twenty-two heavily

[213]

armed men descended from the hut without firing a shot.

That watchtower controlled the entrance to the compound where the prisoners were held. The way seemed clear then to set the prisoners free

Maggie Higgins and Sergeant Furst ordered the SS officer assigned to them by the general to sit on the engine hood of the jeep. He obeyed. Then Furst cocked a pistol and gave it to Maggie, telling her to keep it pointed at the officer.

"We don't want any last-minute tricks," Furst said.

She held the pistol firmly, and the SS man sat silently on the engine hood as the jeep moved toward the enclosure. When they reached the main gate, the SS officer opened it at her command.

This was a moment of tremendous triumph for the girl named Marguerite Higgins, who had fought so hard and traveled so far to arrive in this town in Germany, to be the instrument of liberation for thirty thousand tormented prisoners who had lived under the threat of death for so many months of terror.

Their liberation came a little early — because this girl of twenty-four, who had been born in Hong Kong of an Irish-American father and a French mother, had decided to be a reporter who would make history as well as write it.

When the gate of the Dachau camp was opened, the prisoners called out to the American sergeant and the girl in the strange clothes, wanting to know what was happening.

"The Americans are here," said Marguerite Higgins. "You are free."

The prisoners burst forth in an explosion of joy which rolled from the camp like a tidal wave, sweeping everything before it.

Years later, she depicted their ecstasy of freedom in these words:

In the Second World War it was certainly at Dachau that I came closest to physical injury. For the prisoners who limped, ran, and crawled toward us were in a state of joyful but hysterical frenzy. Their ordeals had quite understandably pushed them far beyond the bounds of self-control. It took half an hour before they could be talked out of toting us around the camp on their shoulders. They meant it as a compliment but the sergeant and I both got badly bruised in this process of being toted — and sometimes tossed — from shoulder to shoulder.

In that wild first half hour at the camp it certainly seemed to the sergeant and me that every single one of the thirty thousand prisoners was determined personally to embrace us or shake our hands. And one sight I'll never forget is the moment the liberated prisoners mistook our SS guide — the one we'd placed on the hood of the jeep — for one of their liberators. This SS man had opened the gate for us. So they deduced not illogically that he was on their side. It was weird to see the grimacing, unwilling SS man being toted around as a hero, cheered and applauded. He was soon found out. The last time I saw this SS guard he lay dead outside the prison gates. He had been beaten to death.

Maggie Higgins and Sergeant Furst were greatly relieved when the Forty-second and Forty-fifth American divisions reached the camp, bringing order and discipline to the dancing, shouting, singing prisoners.

An American general was shocked when he saw the girl from the *Herald Tribune* in the camp, surrounded by emaciated men who looked like living skeletons.

She described his reaction in her own vivid way later:

I was in the midst of a crush of prisoners, all demanding to tell me their terrible stories.

"What are you doing in there?" the general shouted. "Don't you know the place is raging with typhus? Come here."

When I reached the main gate, which was made of iron grillwork, he reached through and grabbed me by my shirt collar. He shook me so hard that whatever bits of me hadn't already been shaken by the prisoners were now thoroughly taken care of. I was so astonished and rattled (literally) that it took me some moments to find voice.

I shouted at the top of my lungs, "Lay off. You let go of me. I've had my typhus shots. I'm in here doing my job."

After some further shouting along these lines, he let go. But I think he forgave both me and Sergeant Furst, with whom he also had a go-around (it was only verbal). For later in the afternoon Sergeant Furst and I had occasion to help the Army by taking turns speaking in German over the loudspeaker systems to the prisoners, who had started a riot when they learned that instead of immediate liberation they would have to be quarantined so that they could be screened for typhus.

In the pandemonium the sergeant and I had suddenly remembered that the electric current running through the barbed wire was still on. While I urged calm over the loudspeaker and warned of the danger of electrocution, Sergeant Furst searched through the camp for a technician who knew how to turn off the master switch. He and some Army officer joined forces to see that it was done. But before this happened, and despite our warnings, a half dozen prisoners in suicidal protest against the quarantine edict had flung themselves against the electrically charged fences, electrocuting themselves before our eyes.

The day at Dachau brought both the sergeant and myself the Army campaign ribbon for outstanding service with the armed forces under difficult conditions. I have since been told that the recommendation was made by our erstwhile foe, the brigadier general.

That day of daring also brought Marguerite Higgins her first major award as a reporter — the prize given by the New York Newspaper Women's Club for the best foreign correspondence of 1945.

It was given not simply for her skill and success as a reporter with limitless courage, but also for her participation in the liberation of the thirty thousand prisoners in the grim camp at Dachau — the prisoners who had waited so long for the arrival of the Americans who had come to set Europe free.

17 | William L. Laurence Sees the Atomic Age Arrive in a Blaze of Light

NINETY MEN went hurrying through a starless night in New Mexico, and all of them knew the world was about to change. Their caravan, consisting of three buses and three motor cars and a truck loaded with radio equipment, went secretly and smoothly along the dusty pavement of U. S. Highway 85, through the empty streets of little towns where people slept and did not dream that the earth would be a changed place before many hours had passed. The ninety men in the caravan looked silently at the dark quiet houses of those little towns.

Nearly all of them were scientists from the bomb research and development center northwest of Santa Fe. Nearly all of them were reasonably sure of what was going to happen. The old world would not end when the powers in the atom were set loose. It would be transformed, but it would not end. They were reasonably sure of that.

One of the ninety men was a little apart from the rest. He was with them, he talked with them and they talked with him freely. But he was different, this stocky man with the dark hair and the very serious face, this scholarly-looking man with a notebook.

He was not a scientist, although he understood so much of science that he could speak the language of scientists. He was a reporter who had won their confidence, and the confidence of Lieutenant General Leslie Groves, the military commander of the atomic project. He was William L. Laurence of the *New York Times* — the only reporter who had been allowed to go to all the atomic plants, the only reporter permitted to travel in this caravan to see the first testing of the atomic bomb.

The caravan passed through the little towns with the Spanish names — Los Lunas, Belen, Bernalillo, Socorro. At San Antonio, the vehicles turned east and crossed a bridge, and then turned south on a newly constructed dirt road.

After traveling about five miles on this road, the caravan came to a line of silent soldiers with steel helmets. Beyond these guards were military police, who carefully checked the special credentials each of the ninety men possessed.

When their credentials had been verified, they were

able to climb from their vehicles. There was not much to see. The night was without stars, and the heavy clouds overhead were illuminated only briefly by flashes of lightning along the eastern edge of the sky.

The lightning showed the bleak expanse of the New Mexico desert and that was all. They were far from civilization, far from the inhabited places where people slept peacefully in their homes. They were out on the rim of the world, watching for a sight no men had ever seen before.

Laurence saw the beam of a searchlight coming from the southeast, touching the thick clouds. He knew that the bomb-testing site, Zero, was a little to the left of the beam, about twenty miles away. He stood on the slope of a hill with the group of scientists. From here, his view of the test would be excellent.

If the bomb worked as it was supposed to work, he would not be in any great danger. If something went wrong, if the explosion created havoc over an area much vaster than it was supposed to damage, he might be annihilated with the other witnesses. But he did not expect that. He had faith in the calculations of the men in charge of the project.

The scientists formed a circle to listen to the instructions on what they were required to do when the blast occurred. With a flashlight pointed at the in-struction sheets, one man read aloud the precautions they were to take.

Five minutes before the moment of zero — the moment of explosion — they would hear a brief wailing of a siren. If their duties permitted, they were to prepare a place on which they could lie prone.

At two minutes before zero, there would be a long sounding of the siren. If possible, they were then supposed to stretch out on the ground, face down, lying with their heads away from the direction of the blast.

They were not to watch the flash with direct glances, but were to roll over after it had occurred. Then they could watch the cloud which would be rising from the bomb site.

No one was supposed to rise from the ground until the blast wave had passed. This would be about two minutes after the explosion. Two brief cries from the siren would give them notice that all dangers from the flash and the blast were considered to be over, and they would then prepare to leave as soon as possible.

Laurence recorded all these details in the book he wrote later, called *Dawn Over Zero:*

David Dow, assistant to the scientific director of the Atomic Bomb Development Center, handed each man a flat piece of colored glass such as arc welders use.

Dr. Edward Teller of George Washington University

cautioned us against the possibility of sunburn. Someone passed sunburn lotion around. It was eerie to see high scientists rubbing the lotion on their faces and hands in the dark night, twenty miles from the expected flash.

After the suntan lotion had been applied, most of the witnesses had nothing to do. The explosion was scheduled for 5:30 A.M., mountain war time, on the morning of July 16. In the hours after midnight, the New Mexico desert grew cold. Many of the men, who were wearing light summer clothing, began to shiver.

Some of them paced up and down, beating their hands together. Some walked slowly back and forth, staring off through the darkness toward the bomb site.

The bomb was placed on a structural steel tower one hundred feet high. In the control center, prepared to operate the master robots which would activate other robots and finally set off the explosion, were Dr. J. Robert Oppenheimer, the scientist in charge, and his field commander, Professor Kenneth T. Bainbridge of Harvard.

Slowly the hours passed. The clouds overhead remained threatening, and occasionally a drizzling rain fell. The scientists and Laurence on the observation hill huddled around a radio which carried reports from the control center.

Laurence knew there was a possibility that the test explosion might be postponed because of weather conditions. He looked up toward the dark sky, knowing that two specially equipped B-29's were flying over the area, making observations and recordings in the upper atmosphere. But he could not see or hear them.

As the time dragged by, the men on the hill grew taut with tension. Many of them had contributed, in one way or another, to the building of the equipment which had made the bomb's development possible. Now the years of frustration and frantic effort were almost over. Now the moment was near when they would know whether the United States had won the race to be the first nation to release the enormous energy in the atom.

Suddenly a voice came through the darkness. The radio spoke:

"Zero minus ten seconds!"

Laurence saw a green flare shoot out through the clouds, fall slowly, grow faint, and disappear. He heard the voice call again: "Zero minus three seconds!"

He watched another green flare rise and fall. Then there was a terrible stillness in the desert. Off to the east, there were the first streaks of grayness, the hints of dawn.

And then Laurence saw it — the most tremendous sight in the history of civilized man — the blaze of light from the rending of the very structure of matter, a fire from the core of the world's substance.

He described it later as a light "not of this world, the light of many suns in one."

He wrote:

It was a sunrise such as the world had never seen, a great green super-sun climbing in a fraction of a second to a height of more than 8000 feet, rising ever higher until it touched the clouds, lighting up earth and sky all around with a dazzling luminosity.

Up it went, a great ball of fire about a mile in diameter, changing colors as it kept shooting upward, from deep purple to orange, expanding, growing bigger, rising as it expanded, an elemental force freed from its bonds after being chained for billions of years.

And after the fire came the thunder — a rumble of gigantic booming. The earth quivered. A wave of hot wind swept over the hill where the witnesses watched.

One of the men near Laurence, Professor George Kistiakowsky of Harvard, said to him, "It was the nearest thing to doomsday that one could possibly imagine. I am sure that at the end of the world — in the last millisecond of the earth's existence — the last man will see what we have just seen!"

But Laurence thought it might be the dawn of a new day for mankind, not a doomsday at all. He shared the exuberance of the scientists, who leaped to their feet and broke into a wild dance on the hill — shaking hands, clapping backs, shouting with joy.

The freeing of atomic energy on such a scale opened endless possibilities for the future — in knowledge of the universe, in power to travel to other planets, in the science of medicine, in a thousand fields of man's work. Laurence knew that this power would probably be used in war — but the war would end and the achievements made possible by atomic energy would go on for centuries, for ages to come.

Less than a month after the successful test of the atom bomb in the New Mexico desert, the power of this new weapon was used against two Japanese cities — Hiroshima and Nagasaki. Laurence was in one of the planes which made the raid on Nagasaki. Once again, he had a complete scoop. He was the only reporter allowed to make the flight.

In his dispatch describing the bombing of Nagasaki, Laurence brought out the role of changing winds which saved another Japanese city from destruction.

He wrote, in an article printed September 9, 1945, in the *New York Times,* but datelined August 9 — the day of the bombing:

> Somewhere beyond these vast mountains of white clouds ahead of me there lies Japan, the land of our enemy.
>
> In about four hours from now one of its cities, making

weapons of war for use against us, will be wiped off the map by the greatest weapon ever made by man.

In one tenth of a millionth of a second, a fraction of time immeasurable by any clock, a whirlwind from the skies will pulverize thousands of its buildings and tens of thousands of its inhabitants.

But at this moment no one knows which one of the several cities chosen as targets is to be annihilated. The final choice lies with destiny. The winds over Japan will make the decision. If they carry heavy clouds over our primary target, that city will be saved, at least for the time being. None of its inhabitants will ever know that the wind of a benevolent destiny had passed over their heads. But that same wind will doom another city. Our weather planes ahead of us are on their way to find out where the wind blows. Half an hour before target time we will know what the winds have decided.

Does one feel any pity or compassion for the poor devils about to die? Not when one thinks of Pearl Harbor and of the Death March on Bataan.

The plane in which Laurence flew circled several times about the city originally chosen as a primary target, but could not find an opening in the clouds. Clouds also protected other cities, Laurence wrote.

The winds of destiny seemed to favor certain Japanese cities that must remain nameless. . . . Destiny chose Nagasaki as the ultimate target.

The bombing flight consisted of three planes — *The Great Artiste,* which carried an atom bomb, and two escort B-29's, including the one in which Laurence rode.

At one minute after noon, the planes arrived over Nagasaki. There was an opening in the clouds. The city was doomed.

Laurence wrote:

We heard the prearranged signal on our radio, put on our arc welder's glasses, and watched tensely the maneuverings of the strike ship about half a mile in front of us.

"There she goes!" someone said.

Out of the belly of *The Great Artiste* what looked like a black object went downward.

Captain Bock swung around to get out of range; but even though we were turning away in the opposite direction, and despite the fact that it was broad daylight in our cabin, all of us became aware of a giant flash that broke through the dark barrier of our arc welder's glasses and flooded our cabin with intense light. . . .

Observers in the tail of our ship saw a giant ball of fire arise as though from the bowels of the earth, belching forth enormous white smoke rings. Next they saw a giant pillar of purple fire, ten thousand feet high, shooting skyward with enormous speed.

By the time our ship had made another turn in the direction of the atomic explosion the pillar of purple fire had reached the level of our altitude. Only about forty-five seconds had passed. Awe-struck, we watched it shoot upward like a meteor coming from the earth instead of from outer space, becoming ever more alive as it climbed skyward through the white clouds. It was no longer smoke, or dust, or even a cloud of fire. It was a living thing, a new species of being, born right before our incredulous eyes.

There in the bomber above Japan, Laurence saw the thing go through many changes:

At one stage of its evolution, covering millions of years in terms of seconds, the entity assumed the form of a giant square totem pole, with its base about three miles long, tapering off to about a mile at the top. Its bottom was brown, its center was amber, and its top white. But it was a living totem pole, carved with many grotesque masks grimacing at the earth.

Then, just when it appeared as though the thing had settled down into a state of permanence, there came shooting out of the top a giant mushroom that increased the height of the pillar to a total of forty-five thousand feet. The mushroom top was even more alive than the pillar, seething and boiling in a white fury of creamy foam, sizzling upward and then descending earthward, a thousand Old Faithful geysers rolled into one.

It kept struggling in an elemental fury, like a creature in the act of breaking the bonds that held it down. In a few seconds it had freed itself of its gigantic stem and floated upward with tremendous speed, its momentum carrying it into the stratosphere to a height of about sixty thousand feet.

But no sooner did this happen when another mushroom, smaller in size than the first one, began emerging out of the pillar. It was as though the decapitated monster was growing a new head.

As the first mushroom floated off into the blue, it changed its shape into a flowerlike form, its giant petals curving downward, creamy white outside, rose-colored inside. It still retained that shape when we last gazed at it from a distance of about two hundred miles.

The boiling pillar of many colors could also be seen at that distance, a giant mountain of jumbled rainbows, in travail. Much living substance had gone into those rainbows.

The quivering top of the pillar was protruding to a great height through the white clouds, giving the appearance of a monstrous prehistoric creature with a ruff around its neck, a fleecy ruff extending in all directions, as far as the eye could see.

That was the thing which destroyed the city of Nagasaki — as it looked to William L. Laurence and the men in the plane flying above the clouds.

For his work in reporting the explosion at Nagasaki and ten articles on the bomb's development, Laurence was given a Pulitzer Prize — the second such prize he had won for outstanding reporting. He witnessed some of the most astounding events in man's history, and he described them vividly and honestly.

18 | Hal Boyle Helps to Save a Child in the Burning Capital of Korea

THE BIG MAN with the broad Irish face bounced along in the jeep, sitting silently beside his companion, who drove carefully through the firelit streets of the flaming city of Seoul. The flickering glow of the flames made everything seem shadowy and shimmering. Sometimes the glow was very bright and hot, and the fires roared hoarsely. Sometimes they plunged into zones of absolute blackness, in places the fires had not yet reached.

What a fine target we make silhouetted against the flames, the Irishman named Boyle was thinking, looking at the man with him, the man at the steering wheel. If there are Chinese in those alleys, all they'd need to do would be to give us a burst with a fast gun or throw a grenade; they couldn't miss.

Well, if they try, let them try. He slouched down in his seat and yawned. He was weary in his bones. He had seen too much of war; he couldn't worry about anything any more. He had been in North Africa, Italy, Normandy, Belgium, Germany, too many places.

The tanks and guns of the retreating United Nations army were rumbling around him, hurrying toward the bridges south of Seoul, abandoning the ancient capital of Korea in the path of a human avalanche — the grim, sad men from Communist China. It was the night of January 3, 1951, and the Korean people were in the grip of the worst agony they had suffered. The Red Chinese were upon them like a plague of locusts.

It seemed to the big Irishman, Hal Boyle of the Associated Press, that the Koreans had gone through more terrible things than any other people on the face of the earth. The Koreans had nothing left to them but the rags they walked in.

And yet the Koreans were a singing people, a smiling people, a people full of laughter and song. The Koreans could sing when other people might have broken down and wept. The Koreans went on singing and enduring, with nothing on their backs but rags, nothing to eat but a handful of rice.

He saw them walking from the burning city, pushing wheelbarrows with a few family possessions, carrying children or old men and women. He saw oxcarts loaded and creaking slowly through the night. He saw sons carrying their fathers, daughters carrying their mothers.

And he saw some of them fall and lie face down in the streets, under the dancing shadows cast by the flames. Some of them did not rise again.

He wondered why he had decided to stay with the rear guard in this burning city, why he was riding in a jeep through the freezing January night with another reporter, Dwight Martin of *Time* magazine. With Martin and a few others he had decided to remain and witness Seoul's last hours under the United Nations banner. He did not know why he had stayed — except that it was his job to see everything and tell the world if he could.

For more than eight years now he had been wandering from place to place, hunting stories, writing a column six days a week. He had almost drowned on a coral reef off the coast of North Africa. He had almost been blown to pieces by a bomb at Cassino. He had crawled through fields under shell fire. That was his job, and he did it.

But Korea was heartbreaking. The people had so little to begin with, and they had lost almost everything. They still had a strong spirit, but that was a miracle.

Then Boyle saw the little figure of a small boy sitting on the steps of a large gray building just ahead of the jeep. The boy was outlined by the fires which were devouring the buildings behind him. One small arm was raised, and Boyle realized that the boy was crying.

It was rare for Koreans to cry. But this little boy

seemed to be totally lost. No one was near him. He sat all alone on the steps, one fist knuckling into his right eye, tears streaming down his cheeks.

"Let's pick him up," Boyle said. Martin nodded and stopped the jeep.

Boyle climbed the steps and lifted the boy into his arms. In the firelight, the boy was sobbing with grief and despair.

The little boy wore a small fur cap, some scraps of clothes that seemed to have been made from fragments of an American uniform, and a pair of torn boots. He was shivering. His feet were icy.

The boy had a round face, painted rosy by the red light of the fires. He had big, expressive dark eyes. His hair was cut close to his scalp. He looked half like a devil, half like an angel, Boyle thought.

Boyle got back into the jeep.

"He's cold," Boyle said.

"We might get some blankets at the hotel," Martin said.

They drove to the Hotel Chosun. It had been evacuated by the UN forces. It was empty and full of the crackling echoes of nearby fires. But they found some blankets.

Boyle wrapped blankets around the boy, covered the torn boots, got the small feet warm. The jeep drove on through the night, through the city of smoke and fire.

With the boy in his arms, Boyle sat thinking of the thousands of orphans roaming the roads of Korea — the pitiful children who were the tragic victims of war. In all his experience, in Africa and Italy and France and Germany, he had never seen so many homeless children.

It was especially terrible to see orphans in Korea, because the Koreans had such a warm family life. The Koreans loved children — children were the only wealth they had. Yet this war had killed so many civilians, so many parents had been slaughtered, that thousands of Korean families had been shattered.

Boyle and his wife had wanted a child for a long time, but they had none. He thought this Korean boy might be the one he ought to keep. He hoped he could keep this boy, the boy he had found sitting alone and abandoned in the midst of fires.

The jeep came to the command post at the southern edge of Seoul. Some American soldiers were opening Christmas packages which had just arrived from the United States. They gave the boy some slices of fruit-cake from America.

Boyle and Martin and the little Korean boy slept that night on the floor in the command post. The boy snuggled down under a mound of blankets.

The next morning, the last units of the UN forces

moved out of Seoul. Many of the men in those units believed the Chinese avalanche would sweep the UN troops into the sea. Some were full of futile anger and despair.

But the Korean boy was cheerful and lively as a cricket. The terror of the night seemed to have been forgotten.

When Boyle lifted him into the jeep, the boy gave a happy laugh. To be in an American jeep, with two big Americans, was a tremendous pleasure. His eyes told them that.

The jeep was one of the last vehicles to cross the remaining bridge south of Seoul. Soon after it had passed over the span, the bridge was blown up by American engineers.

The Korean boy was not dismayed. He lifted his voice in two songs. One may have been taught to him by American missionaries, the other by American soldiers.

He sang, "Oh, my darling, oh, my darling, oh, my darling Clementine," in a clear bright voice, over and over.

And then he looked at Boyle and Martin, and he sang softly:

> *"Jesus loves me! this I know,*
> *For the Bible tells me so."*

When the jeep reached the press camp at the provisional capital of South Korea, in the city called Taegu, the small Korean was given a bed and allowed to stay with the American correspondents. One of the reporters gave him a name — Charlie Company — that seemed to fit him.

Boyle took him to a bootmaker in Taegu and had a fine pair of red boots made for him. The little boy followed the big Irishman everywhere, and Boyle learned that the boy referred to him as "my American."

The UN forces formed a new battle line and stopped the Chinese. Then the United Nations army gathered additional strength, mainly from the United States, and marched up the Korean peninsula to recapture much of the ground that had been lost.

The time came for Hal Boyle to return to the United States. He had learned that Charlie Company's parents had been killed in a bombing, and he wanted to adopt the boy and take him home to America. The boy was quick and bright, and he believed Charlie could easily learn the ways of the United States.

But an Air Force chaplain convinced Boyle that the boy should stay in the country of his ancestors. The boy would always feel out of place in America, the chaplain said. The boy should stay in Korea and help his country recover from the devastation of the war.

On the day of Boyle's departure, the boy rode with him to the airport in the company of another American. Boyle had not told Charlie that he was going back to the United States. He could not bring himself to tell the boy.

He knew the boy would get good care in a Korean orphanage. He knew that the gap between the Korean way of life and the American way was very great, and Charlie would have suffered if he had tried to make the boy bridge that gap. But he hated to leave the child.

When he got in to the plane, he looked at the little figure standing so bravely on the field, and he knew that Charlie had the strength and the courage to grow up into a fine man. Yet Charlie had known so much sorrow — too much grief for a little boy to bear. It was hard to leave the boy behind.

The plane rose in the sky and the big Irishman looked down at the dwindling figure, and he thought of that freezing night when he had seen the little figure outlined against the firelight in that scarred city of Seoul. And he wished he had a child. He wished he had the boy with him.

Then he remembered Charlie singing in the jeep while the bridge was being blown up over the river, and he remembered the high, piping voice singing, "Oh, my darling, oh, my darling, oh, my darling Clementine," and singing:

> *"Jesus loves me! this I know,*
> *For the Bible tells me so."*

And he knew Charlie would be all right. Charlie had come through fire and freezing weather, the loss of a home, the loss of a father and a mother, and Charlie could still sing.

Bibliography

Following are the books consulted most often by the author in preparing this volume:

Daniel Defoe: A Study in Conflict, by Brian Fitzgerald. Secker & Warburg, London, 1954. Henry Regnery Co., Chicago, 1955.

The Incredible Defoe, by William Freeman. Herbert Jenkins, London, 1950.

Life of Samuel Johnson, by James Boswell. Everyman's Library, 1925.

Samuel Johnson, by Joseph Wood Krutch. Henry Holt & Co., New York, 1944.

Life of Charles Dickens, by John Forster. D. Appleton & Co., 1880.

Dickens: His Character, Comedy and Career, by Hesketh Pearson. Harper & Bros., 1949.

How I Found Livingstone, by Henry M. Stanley. Scribner's, New York, 1913.

Mark Twain: A Biography, by Albert Bigelow Paine. Harper & Bros., 1912.

The Ordeal of Mark Twain, by Van Wyck Brooks. E. P. Dutton & Co., 1920.

Autobiography, by Mark Twain. Harper & Bros., 1924.

[241]

Nellie Bly's Book, by Elizabeth Cochrane. Pictorial Weeklies Co., 1890.

This Is London, by Edward R. Murrow. Simon & Schuster, 1941.

Here Is Your War, by Ernie Pyle. Henry Holt & Co., 1943.

The Story of Ernie Pyle, by Lee Miller. Viking Press, 1950.

Dawn Over Zero, by William L. Laurence. A. A. Knopf, 1946.

Stephen Crane, by Thomas Beer. A. A. Knopf, 1926.

Stephen Crane, by John Berryman. William Sloane Associates, 1950.

A Roving Commission, by Winston Churchill. Scribner's, 1940.

Winston Churchill, by Robert Lewis Taylor. Doubleday, 1952.

Ladies of the Press, by Ishbel Ross. Harper & Bros., 1936.

Floyd Gibbons, by Edward Gibbons. Exposition Press, 1953.

With the Allies, by Richard Harding Davis. Scribner's, 1914.

Richard Harding Davis, by Fairfax Downey. Scribner's, 1933.

Men at War (Introduction by Ernest Hemingway). Crown, 1942.

Ernest Hemingway, by Philip Young. Rinehart, 1952.

The Apprenticeship of Ernest Hemingway, by Charles A. Fenton. Farrar, Straus & Cudahy, 1954.

News Is a Singular Thing, by Marguerite Higgins. Doubleday, 1954.

Star Reporters and 34 of Their Stories, by Ward Greene. Random House, 1948.

A Treasury of Great Reporting, by Louis L. Snyder and Richard B. Morris. Simon & Schuster, 1949.